# THE QUEST FOR
# LEARNING

## How to **MAXIMIZE** Student Engagement

Marie **ALCOCK**   Michael **FISHER**   Allison **ZMUDA**

*foreword by Heidi Hayes Jacobs*

Solution Tree | Press

555 North Morton Street
Bloomington, IN 47404
800.733.6786 (toll free) / 812.336.7700
FAX: 812.336.7790

email: info@SolutionTree.com
SolutionTree.com

Visit **go.SolutionTree.com/instruction** to download the free reproducibles in this book.

Printed in the United States of America

21   20   19   18   17                    1   2   3   4   5

Library of Congress Cataloging-in-Publication Data

Names: Alcock, Marie, author. | Fisher, Michael L., author. | Zmuda, Allison, author.
Title: The quest for learning : how to maximize student engagement / Marie Alcock, Michael Fisher, and Allison Zmuda.
Description: Bloomington, IN : Solution Tree Press, [2018] | Includes bibliographical references and index.
Identifiers: LCCN 2017015293 | ISBN 9781942496908 (perfect bound)
Subjects: LCSH: Inquiry-based learning. | Individualized instruction. | Effective teaching. | Engagement (Philosophy)
Classification: LCC LB1027.23 .A56 2018 | DDC 370.15/23--dc23 LC record available at https://lccn.loc.gov/2017015293

**Solution Tree**
Jeffrey C. Jones, CEO
Edmund M. Ackerman, President

**Solution Tree Press**
*President and Publisher:* Douglas M. Rife
*Editorial Director:* Sarah Payne-Mills
*Art Director:* Rian Anderson
*Managing Production Editor:* Caroline Cascio
*Senior Production Editor:* Tonya Maddox Cupp
*Senior Editor:* Amy Rubenstein
*Copy Editors:* Miranda Addonizio and Ashante K. Thomas
*Proofreader:* Jessi Finn
*Text and Cover Designer:* Laura Cox
*Editorial Assistants:* Jessi Finn and Kendra Slayton

*To our professional parents—Heidi Hayes Jacobs, Bena Kallick, Jay McTighe, and Grant Wiggins. Your expertise, love, and collaboration have left an indelible impression on who we are and continue to inspire our pedagogical quests. There is no better affinity space to be a part of, and we humbly thank you.*

# Acknowledgments

*The Quest for Learning: How to Maximize Student Engagement* is the product of a journey we began when we realized we shared a deep dedication to the joy in learning, the learners themselves, and the art of teaching. The quest we went on together had moments of magic, hydra heads, and heroism. We now have a fellowship forged by the unbreakable bonds of writing together, learning together, and questing together. It has been the greatest honor and privilege to travel as a company of colleagues and friends.

To the greatest heroes we know—our families. Thank you.

From Marie, to my family, Jim, Garret, Colin, and Isabelle. Your love and support for me through my learning and writing make any and all of this possible. My deepest gratitude and love are yours.

From Michael, to my family, Liz, Lily, and Charlotte. Thank you once again for allowing me to indulge my interests and supporting me as I spend nights, early mornings, and weekends writing. I've said it before and I'll say it again, "I'll be off the computer in five minutes!"

From Allison, to my family, Tom, Zoe, and Cuda. I appreciate your patience with me during the writing process as well as your coaching me through multiple new games. Thank you for your love and support.

There were other heroes along the way. In particular, we want to thank the multitude of people who read bits and snippets of this text and provided feedback, namely Bena Kallick, Jay McTighe, and Jesse Schell. Thank you to those who allowed us to try ideas out in their districts. We are especially thankful to Kathy Schuessler, Sheila Murphy, Mickey Edwards, Evelyn Russo, Maureen Ruby, Andrea Meiers, Susan von Felten, Dana Watts, Linda Anderson, Don Drake, Suanne Forrester, Arcia Dorosti, Paul Negrete, Carol Campbell, Izett Thomas, Davenia Lea, Catherine Addor, and Brian Durst.

We are deeply grateful to Heidi Hayes Jacobs for her gracious and insightful foreword. As a thought leader in the areas of curriculum development and contemporary schools, she continues to inspire us and our entire profession.

Thank you to our editors, Tonya Maddox Cupp and Rayna Penning, for their insight, patience, and support. They both worked shoulder to shoulder with us to make this book happen. We are grateful to Douglas M. Rife for the opportunity to work together. Finally, to the learners who allowed us and continue inviting us to join them on their quests for learning—thank you.

Solution Tree Press would like to thank the following reviewers:

Dave Bircher
Principal
Wolseley High School
Wolseley, Saskatchewan
Canada

Brian Disney
Principal
Mooresville High School
Mooresville, Indiana

Steve Johnson
Principal
Highland Elementary School
Elgin, Illinois

Saul Laredo
Principal
Dooley Elementary School
Plano, Texas

Karen Moore
Director of 21st Century Curriculum
Orange Schools
Pepper Pike, Ohio

Tamera Steenhoek
PK–12 Literacy Coordinator
Southeast Polk Community School
   District
Pleasant Hill, Iowa

Beth Woof
Principal
Sherwood Secondary School
Hamilton, Ontario
Canada

Visit **go.SolutionTree.com/instruction** to download the free reproducibles in this book.

# Table of Contents

# About the Authors

 **Marie Alcock** is president of Learning Systems Associates, founder of Tomorrow's Education Network, and an educational consultant in the United States and internationally. Marie has worked in public and private education as a teacher, administrator, and public advocate since 1996. Her work focuses on the areas of curriculum, instruction, and assessment.

Marie is a member of the Curriculum21 faculty, the Association for Supervision and Curriculum Development, and the American Educational Research Association. Marie coauthored *Bold Moves for Schools: How We Create Remarkable Learning Environments* and *Mapping to the Core: Integrating the Common Core Standards Into Your Local School Curriculum—Planner* and contributed to *The Power of the Social Brain: Teaching, Learning, and Interdependent Thinking.* Marie is also a contributing author to Solution Tree's *Contemporary Perspectives on Literacy* series and has written a number of papers and articles about student mobility, innovative models of education, curriculum mapping, gaming in education, leadership, and organizational change.

Marie has a doctorate in philosophy from Walden University and a master's degree in the art of education from Marygrove College, and she graduated summa cum laude with a bachelor of arts in social science from Castleton University.

To learn more about Marie's work, visit Learning Systems Associates (www.lsalearning .com), or follow @mariealcock on Twitter.

 **Michael Fisher** is an educational consultant and instructional coach working with schools and districts in the United States and internationally to facilitate curriculum upgrades, design curriculum, and modernize instruction with immersive technology. Previously, Michael taught a variety of grade levels and content areas, working primarily in middle schools.

Michael is a member of both the Association for Supervision and Curriculum Development (ASCD) faculty and the Curriculum21 faculty. He is an active blogger who writes often for the blogs *Curriculum21* and *ASCD EDge*. Michael is the author of *Digital Learning Strategies: How Do I Assign and Assess 21st Century Work?* and *Ditch the Daily Lesson Plan: How Do I Plan for Meaningful Student Learning?* and a coauthor of *Upgrade Your Curriculum: Practical Ways to Transform Units and Engage Students*. He is also a contributing author to Solution Tree's *Contemporary Perspectives on Literacy* series and has written *Hacking the Common Core: 10 Strategies for Amazing Learning in a Standardized World*.

Michael holds a bachelor's degree in biology from the University of North Carolina at Wilmington and a master's degree in English education from Buffalo State College. He also holds post-baccalaureate certificates in teaching science, language arts, and gifted students.

To learn more about Michael's work, visit his website The Digigogy Collaborative (http://digigogy.com) or follow @fisher1000 on Twitter.

 **Allison Zmuda** is a full-time educational consultant specializing in curriculum, instruction, and assessment. She works with clients in the United States and internationally to imagine learning experiences and design work that is relevant, meaningful, challenging, and appropriate. Previously, Allison taught high school social studies for eight years.

She has coauthored nine books, including *Learning Personalized: The Evolution of the Contemporary Classroom*; *Real Engagement: How Do I Help My Students Become Motivated, Confident, and Self-Directed Learners?*; and *Students at the Center: Personalizing Learning With Habits of Mind*. With Bena Kallick, she developed a series of online personalized learning courses.

Allison holds a master of arts in liberal studies in American studies from Wesleyan University and graduated magna cum laude with a bachelor of arts in American studies from Yale University.

To learn more about Allison's work, follow @allison_zmuda on Twitter.

The authors invite you to their affinity space to share the things your students are learning by questing. Use the hashtag #Quest4Learning on Twitter to interact with the authors and other educators.

To book Marie Alcock, Michael Fisher, or Allison Zmuda for professional development, contact pd@SolutionTree.com.

# Foreword

*By Heidi Hayes Jacobs*

Fusion creates new energy, and the integrative force of Alcock, Fisher, and Zmuda in *The Quest for Learning* ignites innovative possibilities for learners and their teachers. But their fusion does more than that. It genuinely shifts pedagogy into fresh territory with regard to approach, time, and motivation. As educators at every level of learning ask, "How can we engage our right-now learners in meaningful queries?" this trio of authors takes a deep dive into this question with creative and powerful results.

In response to that question, the authors compel us to reconsider more rigid views of instructional models and curriculum planning and see the potential for hooking our learners on questing threads both spontaneously and over time. Their carefully crafted tenets of engagement serve as a vibrant questing platform that can drive our professional choices and actions.

I am particularly struck by how Alcock, Fisher, and Zmuda build on these tenets by tackling the challenge of naturally merging three critical contemporary arenas into practice: gaming, networking, and question design. These arenas have perplexed teachers and school leaders who grapple with modern learning experiences. Gaming is a source of fascination and considerable discussion, especially among educators who are involved in game play, but it has remained an outlier in everyday school life and practice. In this book, readers not only explore and compare an array of game types but gain direct connections between gaming and content areas and skills.

Networking is part of everyday life for most students and teachers, yet it conspicuously gets neglected in curriculum planning. Here, the authors open up specific strategies for making discerning networking choices in regard to social-networking platforms, community organizations, in-school networks, and peer relationships.

Also, while raising questions for investigation is not new to educators because it is at the heart of teaching and learning, the authors argue for a more nuanced view of questioning. They propose teachers present questions that provoke student ownership of learning pathways. Respecting each student as unique in a specific place and time, educators must be observant and responsive with the formation of four types of questions that encourage meaningful investigations. In short, the authors declare that because we have contemporary learners, we need to bring those learners to relevant, worthy inquiries and experiences; active, intentional cycles of expertise; and social, collaborative opportunities.

The authors creatively explore examples of gaming, networking, and inquiry. They pack the book with clear visuals showing the relationship between the three arenas, strategies for integrating them, and resources for further exploration.

While reading *The Quest for Learning*, I found it striking how it asks us to think differently about our interactions with students—not only in moment-to-moment interactions but during long-term planning as well. We do not direct learners; we teach them to direct themselves. Questing is a mindset for engagement. Rather than a rigid step-by-step planning model, genuine design thinking is afoot here. Alcock, Fisher, and Zmuda provoke catalytic, genuine rethinking of overly planned, rigid types of inquiry, which contradict the nature of spontaneity. It is not that plans do not matter; they do. But we often miss the myriad of opportunities to actively seek questions, deepen curiosity, and determine which questions merit longer-term investigation.

*The Quest for Learning* cultivates the joys of an epiphany-making environment. The authors walk us through golden opportunities to pick up on student interests and convert them into threads for inquiry. This book is a wake-up call to mindful listening and observation. Often, the clues we need are there—with both motivated and struggling learners.

Timely in its focus, *The Quest for Learning* provides direct guidance for administrators and teachers who are developing personalized learning opportunities. Nationally and internationally, school planning meetings lead to lively, often frustrating discussions about what personalized learning looks like. Is it the same as individualized instruction? Is it differentiation? Is it project-based learning? More than any book I have read before, the book in your hands details how to navigate learners through a compelling personalized learning journey. As co-creators, teachers and learners move from interest to inspiration in framing questions, researching and networking, and developing deliverables for an authentic questing experience. What is more, the authors present suggestions in the context of thoughtfully rendered pedagogy refreshed by the three tenets of engagement.

As we all are keenly aware, a new chapter opens the moment a learner walks into his or her classroom for the first time. Yet, in truth, a student encounters the possibility of a new beginning every time he or she walks into the classroom. We know the magic that shines in the eyes of a lit learner. As educators, we can be discerning and responsive guides assisting our charges make meaning and pose new queries. Contemporary students require fresh approaches matching who they are and the time in which they live. *The Quest for Learning* raises our awareness and fuses modern learning tools to open up options. The word *quest* in the book title aptly reflects our never-ending search as educators to develop exceptional thinkers and human beings.

On a personal note, it has been my great personal and professional pleasure to work with Marie, Mike, and Allison over several decades in a range of settings. I knew each of them separately before they met one another, and I admire their individual expertise. It is moving to have witnessed their interactions over the years. Their brilliance, passion, and ingenuity are evident in this book. There is no doubt that their future contributions will be electric.

# Introduction

*Teaching is an invitational art.* If students are reticent to accept the invitation to learn, it limits their capacity to become more skillful and wiser from learning experiences. You work hard to create the favorable conditions for success in hopes of inspiring learners to engage, examine ideas, and produce works of value—How do you feel about what you are doing? Is it worth your time? You wonder how you can meet students' needs—What should I teach? Who can I ask for help? What exactly is my approach, and why am I choosing to take it? What are students getting out of this unit? But learning is a voluntary endeavor. You cannot force a student to learn. You can change curricula, materials, and physical spaces, yet engaging students boils down to teaching in ways that are effective for the individual learner.

The tenets and designs we provide in this book embrace fresh opportunities. *Questing* is an instructional framework that helps teachers create powerful invitations to all learners through a series of choices. Author Seth Godin (2010) contends that there are really only two things teachers need to teach in school: "how to lead" and "how to solve interesting problems" (p. 61). Questing helps address both by embodying a long, arduous search for something that matters to a learner: the hunt for a vaccine, the hope of life on other planets, the pursuit of world peace, the uncovering of what really happened in history. These experiences can result in student-created and teacher-observed evidence that students have met specific learning goals. It is a journey that primarily students lead. Students determine what they consider worth pursuing and, with a teacher's guidance, how they will pursue it.

A quest begins when teachers invite students into this mindset, revealing learning as it unfolds, versus once when they administer an assessment. What students discover and how they engage are as important as the end product. This approach prepares learners for an unpredictable 21st century world filled with messy, complex problems that often require skills such as critical thinking, collaboration, and innovation along with dispositions such as listening with understanding, having empathy, and striving for accuracy.

The questing framework provides access to two elements that we believe are missing in much of learning: joy and community. It is possible to make joy a primary consideration when designing instruction, and you can facilitate it many ways—providing time and space to pursue something fascinating, introducing the struggle of figuring out something elusive, or recognizing progress, for instance. Sometimes that joy comes from being part of a community. Learners use questing to build or make themselves part of a sincere community of others—networks—who develop ideas, solve problems, and share approaches to benefit that space's members. With aspects of the questing framework, which we help you dive deeply into, the focus is as much on the *experience* as it is on the *learning*. The challenge for teachers is both guiding the process as an invitation and documenting the experience effectively. This is where *The Quest for Learning* comes in.

After the following section discerns questing from other instructional models and frameworks, we will introduce questing and its components and provide an overview of what is in this book.

## Discern Questing From Other Instructional Models and Frameworks

The appetite for an instructional *model* satisfies a craving for something tangible to guide instruction with a linear (or near linear) flow of steps, protocols, and tools. An instructional *framework*, which is what questing offers, does not do this; instead, it clearly defines the elements or choices and then uses those elements or choices consistently as the foundation for future models. Questing naturally nests within the instructional model of personalized learning. Allison Zmuda, Greg Curtis, and Diane Ullman (2015) define *personalized learning* as "a progressively student-driven model in which students deeply engage in meaningful, authentic, and rigorous challenges to demonstrate desired outcomes" (p. 7). Questing is very much in line with personalized learning's purposeful choices about when the teacher takes the lead, when teachers and students co-create, and when students take the lead. Bena Kallick and Allison Zmuda (2017b) explain that the "teacher can turn the volume up or down, amplifying or reducing the amount of student agency as the teacher and students begin to feel more comfortable with student self-direction" (p. 54). Exhibiting this responsiveness and allowing this range are vital as you balance alignment with content standards, exposure to new ideas and ways of thinking, and identified areas for individual student growth.

Three learning models or frameworks may appear similar to questing—(1) individualization, (2) differentiation, and (3) project-based learning—because in them, students have increased control over certain aspects of their learning. *Individualization*, a student-centered framework, helps students own the pace of their learning as they tackle content-related problems. They can move at their own pace through a series of topics and demonstrate mastery when they're ready. The teacher manages the learning by helping establish and monitor timelines, offering consultations when needed, and evaluating performance in light of desired results. However, individualization limits students' control over what problems, questions, and challenges they tackle. In addition, students may not interact much with others. The goal may be more focused on completing a topic than engaging in robust learning experiences.

*Differentiation* allows students' content, process, or product choices, but within the confines of what the teacher offers (which he or she determines based on individual students' readiness, interests, and learning preferences). While offering choice, the learning designs typically are prescribed options or scaffolds that the teacher has vetted for alignment with specific learning goals, preferred ways of working, and scoring methods. The teacher functions as a designer, lead instructor, and evaluator. In addition, the teacher sets the pace and often designs instructional tools (such as centers or stations) to support learners in differentiated ways.

*Project-based learning* engages students in the pursuit of a worthy, challenging question or problem over an extended period of time. The students are responsible for delivering a public presentation, but unlike quests, the teacher is primarily responsible for forming the essential question and task, even if students contribute to the deliverables' design. After the project's launch, the teacher may facilitate ongoing work while relinquishing some control to students.

Quests are based specifically on what students determine is compelling, with few, if any, restrictions, though not necessarily without guidance. Quests are not necessarily monthlong projects, though they can be. A quest can occur during the process of learning a cell's major components, for example. In addition, collaboration is an integral part of questing. While writing this book, we embraced the nonlinear and often messy reality of defining a framework. We understand the limits of working within a framework, including the inability to guarantee that if you follow certain steps, everything will go according to plan. We also understand the desire for exactly that kind of reassurance. But it simply isn't possible with questing, and we address that as well—such as when talking about unexpected outcomes, for example.

## Understand Questing and Its Components

To be sure, questing is not unit or curriculum design. You can employ questing with any unit by paying attention to three engagement tenets. We developed these tenets as a result of the interplay among brain-based research, game-based theory, and lots of learner observation. What we offer in this book clarifies some of the more challenging choices and elements within the questing framework more deeply.

Our three learner engagement tenets follow.

1. The learner engages with relevant, worthy inquiries and experiences that are interesting or emotionally gripping.
2. The learner engages in an active, intentional cycle with clear goals and right-sized, actionable steps.
3. The learner engages in social, collaborative opportunities that grow expertise.

The student and teacher experience engagement tenets through a design type. Both make deliberate design choices in the questing framework. In this book, we focus on (1) question design, (2) game design, and (3) network design. These are not the only designs through which students can quest, but they are the ones with which most teachers struggle.

Any one quest may include any combination of inquiry, game, *and* network design choices. Student and teacher make choices through these design lenses to grow their own expertise. What is relevant and worth investigating? What is interesting or emotionally gripping? What networks should I tap into?

After initially outlining something based on the quester's interests, student and teacher design and redesign the details as the learning journey begins unfolding. Participants address details in a *just-in-time* manner, as they crop up, instead of in advance. This powerfully summarizes 21st century learning: discovering something of interest, working in a space with like-minded participants, and establishing either group or individual goals. Developing a prototype, pursuing social reform, or creating a film takes weeks, perhaps months, and represents possible products or events from a questing experience. Those weeks are filled with discovery, missteps, and wins both big and little. These are questers engaging in the learning process.

## See What This Book Offers

To simply promote an experience and call it a quest does not mean the learner automatically experiences engagement and joyful learning. True questing means teachers encourage problem solvers, creators, and critical thinkers to adapt and grow with content, tools, and resources. To that end, the way a teacher facilitates a quest makes or breaks a student's learning experience.

*The Quest for Learning* helps you build a repository of instructional techniques and approaches that generate and sustain quality questing experiences. We split this book into two parts. Part I (chapters 1 through 5) is about establishing questing's foundations; part II (chapters 6 through 9) is about guiding quests. Chapter 1 clarifies why questing is a compelling method for boosting student engagement. Chapter 2 thoroughly explores the three tenets of engagement and introduces three design lenses. Subsequent chapters dig deeply into each design type as a collection of choices to be made while questing—chapter 3 digs deeper into question design choices, chapter 4 into game design choices, and chapter 5 into network design choices.

Part II puts the components together and shows you how to act on the information. This portion of the book asks that readers follow the sequence it gives. Chapter 6 reveals quest inspiration, goal clarification, curriculum mapping, and final products (known as *deliverables*). Chapter 7 helps you introduce students to questing. Chapter 8 details support provision during journeys, starting with timelines and checklists, which help address the standards required of you. Chapter 9 helps teachers and students decide what deliverables students will generate. Each chapter concludes with a coda to wrap up the most salient points therein. Afterward, appendix A addresses frequently asked *quest*ions, and appendix B offers probing questions that help guide quest decisions.

To showcase how the big picture and fine details support one another in quests, we've chosen one illustrative quest example (on the topic of disease) to show how the details within each chapter add dimension and engagement. Our self-imposed criteria for selecting the topic follow.

*   The topic is applicable for students in various age ranges.
*   Students can pursue the topic through myriad courses and subjects.
*   The problem, challenge, or idea is meaningful and worth the pursuit.

This book helps you use the questing framework in your classroom and incorporate learning standards. It also provides planning and assessment tools. (Visit **go.Solution Tree.com/instruction** to download free reproducibles, including an example of the completed disease quest.)

We sincerely hope that you get the following from this book.

*   Inspiration to use questing as a framework in your own classroom
*   Opportunities to seek increased co-creation, win states, affinity spaces, and authentic deliverables
*   Additional tools for your instructional toolbox (including question design options, game design options, and network design options)
*   Tenets of engagement participation options for all students

Pause for a moment to respond to the following questions: What do you want on behalf of your learners? How do you model that, live that, and grow in that space together with your students? This response is a quest's start and guiding reason. We designed this reading experience to examine current realities and grow from them through questioning, imagining, and—most important—taking action. Learning often requires a timeless and courageous act of becoming. This book is the beginning of a conversation. Let's get started.

PART I
# Establishing

# Making the Case for Questing

Dated approaches to school subjects where "problems are solved not by observing and responding to the natural landscape but by mastering time-tested routines, conveniently placed along the path" are ebbing away in favor of more contemporary tactics (National Research Council, 1990, p. 4). A 2016 Gallup report reveals that just 49 percent of students in grades 5 and up feel engaged in school. While facts and skills are still important, they are not akin to information where knowledge is organized around important ideas and concepts and the expectation is that students are examining deeply to determine generalizations, connections, and patterns (Bransford, Brown, & Cocking, 2000). Engagement increases when teachers introduce and students pursue quests. Teachers design them to become increasingly student driven as they progress. While the teacher and student clarify the *why*, the student takes a much more significant role in developing *what* to learn and *how* to demonstrate that learning.

This chapter examines the realities of sit-and-get learning or lower-level thinking such as Benjamin Bloom's (1956) *remember* and *understand* in many classrooms and explains why questing, which requires *apply* and *evaluate*, is preferable. To begin questing, teachers can tap into what moves students and tie those topics into the required standards to increase engagement, embrace technology, and build a community of learners.

## Bypass Sit-and-Get Pedagogy

In 1930, students were being prepared for jobs that valued a command-and-obey structure with clear hierarchies. In 2017, employers lament that students struggle to think, create, and problem solve because of lack of school experience and training (Breene, 2016). Because the post–World War II factory boom has evolved into another kind of global job market, virtually every job, blue and white collar, requires employees to regularly solve a range of intellectual and technical problems (Wagner, 2010). Some blame the absence of problem solving and creativity on a "general lack of curiosity" (Wagner, 2010, p. xxiii). A lack of curiosity might explain so little engagement, as might a linear, teacher-led process filled with content acquisition. Because people can easily access information, they no longer have to memorize it for retrieval. The sit-and-get pedagogy favors isolated academic experiences and progress in tight sequence.

Students can feel at a loss when these important small parts do not connect to broader concepts or applications. For instance, when students memorize words for weekly spelling tests, the words are isolated. There is no connection to bigger ideas or related texts. Students wonder *why* teachers compel them to memorize the words. Worse, they grow accustomed to passively receiving assignments that someone else designed and content curated completely. They may participate in completing the assignments, but are not engaged.

This book is a sort of macroscope, as opposed to a microscope, for looking at the learning process. With this macroscope, you can see connections between our content and ideas. A questing framework offers both—specific content and skills instruction as well as empowering, purposeful learning experiences. There is no need to decide between ensuring coverage and digging deep into Bloom's (1956) higher-level-thinking skills of applying and evaluating.

It is time for schooling to distinguish itself from a culture that required seat time, regimented curriculum pace, and relentless standardized testing. Questing is a solid step toward a more responsive learning experience that encourages curiosity, creativity, and problem solving.

## Increase Engagement

Teachers need their students' hearts and minds when they teach the curriculum. The challenge is how to create the favorable conditions for that attention that is in line with what we know about the brain. Neural connections and long-term memories result when teachers combine emotionally compelling classwork and personal relevance (Bernard, 2010). Research proves that "choice plays a critical role in promoting students' intrinsic motivation and deep engagement in learning" (Evans & Boucher, 2015).

*How* learners feel about the learning also relates to their likelihood of engaging and further development. Neuroscientist Lila Davachi and her colleagues Tobias Kiefer, David Rock, and Lisa Rock (2010) describe this as being in a *toward state* or an *away state*. At the neurological level, the brain perceives what's happening in the moment and classifies it as good (students want to move *toward* it and engage) or bad (students want to move *away* from it and disengage). We can describe the toward state as *active learning* because it's building and reinforcing neurological pathways (Davachi et al., 2010). When a teacher helps students discover connections, students feel more creative and have a greater capacity to stick with something or tackle new problems. The converse can be said when the brain is in the away state, because the brain focuses on following directions. The away response occurs when people cannot connect to previous knowledge, feel no sense of autonomy, do not feel part of a group, or have their status threatened. This is why spending time and attention on the *why* and *how we think and work together*—questing essentials—increases the likelihood students will engage.

# Shift Toward Technology

Computer use varies widely by nation, but over 50 percent of students have access to classroom computers in countries around the world (Organisation for Economic Co-operation and Development, 2012). In U.S. elementary and middle schools, 31 percent of students use a digital device that the school supplies. A full third of high schoolers use school-provided technology, whether it's to research, communicate with teachers or other students, take tests online, or photograph deliverables (Project Tomorrow, 2013). Despite the *digital divide*, or many schools' continued lack of access, technology use seems to be trending upward in classrooms and in education generally. A 2012 Interactive Educational Systems Design survey shows just over 50 percent of participants using mobile technology; a follow-up survey in 2014 shows that 71 percent of participants use mobile technology (as cited in STEMReports, 2014).

A tremendous infusion of technology in schools has changed what, when, where, and with whom we learn. Technology also changes how we demonstrate learning (Zmuda et al., 2015). This digital proliferation stems from teachers providing access to information and global educational opportunities as well as from students being raised in a culture of ubiquitous touch screens and online applications (Mitra, 2010).

Generation Z, born between 1995 and 2009, and Generation Alpha, born after 2010, use technology not only to retrieve information but also to entertain themselves and learn. Students from these generations perceive effective classrooms differently than their predecessors (McCrindle, 2014). Table 1.1 reveals those differences.

**Table 1.1: Differences in Effective Engagement**

| Generation Z and Generation Alpha | Previous Generations |
|---|---|
| Visual | Verbal |
| Try and see | Sit and listen |
| Facilitator | Teacher |
| Flexibility | Security |
| Collaborating | Commanding |
| Learner centered | Curriculum centered |
| Open-book assessments | Closed-book exams |
| Touch technology and electronic devices | Books and paper |

*Source: Adapted from McCrindle, 2014.*

The shift from keyboard to touch interface changed learners. Students expect to interact with content and people differently than previous generations did. They seek, process, and share information more visually, collaboratively, and in real time. What better motivation for questing's instructional framework, which naturally puts teachers *and* students in the driver's seat.

Effective questing involves others. Collaboration via networking is possible in physical interactions, but being able to use digital tools for virtual learning connections is essential. Without the increasingly available connected tools and devices, students will not be adequately prepared.

## Collaborate in Learning Spaces

Social networks also have a significant impact on learning. Neural activity increases when a learner perceives group context and connection (Demolliens, Isbaine, Takerkart, Huguet, & Boussaoud, 2017). Education professors James Paul Gee and Elisabeth Hayes (2011) promote the necessity of an *affinity space*—a learning environment where like-minded learners want to figure out something and pool their talents and resources to do so. Affinity spaces come in two levels—(1) member and (2) mentor—and exist in two shared space types—(1) virtual and (2) physical. This affinity space includes:

> The whole continuum of people from the new to the experienced, from the unskilled to the highly skilled, from the slightly interested to the addicted, and everything in between, [and] is accommodated in the same space where people can pursue different goals within the space, based on their own choices, purposes, and identities. (Gee, 2007, p. 11)

Teachers, peers, and invested members all occupy these affinity spaces, and they play crucial parts in questing. How students relate to teachers and peers will change during a quest because the process reimagines teachers' status quo role as experts and students' as exclusively learners. In these spaces, students learn, receive feedback, and garner assessment from all participants, not just teachers. Students invite expertise from teachers in these spaces, but they also look to affinity space networks (see chapter 2, page 13) to help design and refine questions, seek opportunities to emulate experts, request and provide feedback, and create increasingly higher-quality deliverables. For the brain's need for group connection, among other reasons, questing employs networks. A sincere community of learners promotes engagement and active learning.

## Coda

*Sit-and-get* schooling has run its course. Making space for quests—open-ended opportunities driven by student interest engagement opportunities—can result in active learning, increased engagement, and increased brain activity. Questing can help students become emotionally attached to their learning, driving initiative and self-direction. They are leveraging technology to seek out affinity space members to collaborate with on authentic problems, challenges, and ideas.

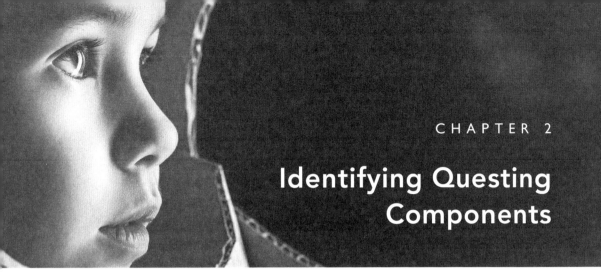

# CHAPTER 2

# Identifying Questing Components

Quests contain a myriad of elements—design approaches, affinity spaces, research types, and products. What is a quest's bedrock? The tenets of engagement. They are true for any learner in any learning condition. Beyond the tenets, there is the element of design to consider. In this book, starting with this chapter, we focus on three contemporary design options that can help maximize these tenets of engagement: (1) inquiry, (2) game, and (3) network. These tenets are interconnected, and any design option you choose might touch any one or all three of them to promote a learner's engagement.

## Tenets of Engagement

These tenets come from a meta-analysis of brain-based research (Kolb, 1984; Zull, 2002), game-based theory (Gee, 2007), and our combined experiences with thousands of students. The tenets speak to the challenging, joyful process of learning regardless of the environment where the learning takes place—at an internship location, in a virtual chat room, during pretend play, or in a laboratory, for example.

The questing framework gives rise to students who are fully engaged, motivated, and committed, persevering through problems with their learning networks and demonstrating expertise—all of which promote the tenets of engagement. As noted in the introduction, these are the three tenets of engagement.

1. The learner engages with relevant, worthy inquiries and experiences that are interesting or emotionally gripping.
2. The learner engages in an active, intentional cycle with clear goals and right-sized, actionable steps.
3. The learner engages in social, collaborative opportunities that grow expertise.

The tenets are not isolated aspirations; teachers, by following and emulating examples in this book, incorporate and grow these tenets throughout instruction to maximize engagement. Nor do they occur linearly. We stress that the tenets can occur in any order, happen repeatedly, or be omitted when appropriate—the choices are yours and your learners'. Let us look more closely at each tenet to examine the research, further explain the significance, and provide examples.

## Relevant, Worthy Inquiries and Experiences

The first tenet is that the learner engages with relevant, worthy inquiries and experiences that are interesting or emotionally gripping. As a teacher, you may deem an inquiry topic worthy if it is motivational, meaningful, or joyful for the student. Science proves that long-term memory and passion for learning increase when students (with help from teachers, if necessary) connect to something that matters to them and they're allowed to choose to pursue that interest (Bernard, 2010; Davachi et al., 2010; Evans & Boucher, 2015). Learners become motivated to try, believing a topic is a valid investment of their time and energy (Lambert, Gong, & Harrison, 2016).

Problem posing and critical thinking are vital here, since students must form questions and conclusions before and throughout their quests. The learner's inquiries stem from his or her sense of curiosity and critical thinking, which stimulates action, conversation, and reflection. For example, elementary students may be interested in designing something to beautify their community. Instead of brainstorming good ideas in a vacuum, they collaborate with the people who will ultimately see the beautification on a daily basis and discover their concerns, challenges, and hopes for the space. Students then use that information to make an inquiry such as, How can we make something that has what people want and involve them in the making?

Another example might be high school students investigating and potentially acting on the global refugee crisis. When discussing current events in class, students may be aghast at the hardships refugees endure. They also may be sympathetic to the rights of sovereign nations that want to be compassionate but do not want to become flooded with new challenges. The questions that emerge are complex: Why are refugees being treated this way, and what can we do to help? Students investigate and collaborate with global organizations such as UNICEF and the United Nations, as well as national and local groups, to provide refugee assistance and examine the real fears people have when they see a new wave of refugees.

The beautification and refugee examples are a testament that student inquiries can drive a quest at the same time they address key standards. Elementary and middle school students can interview neighbors (speaking and listening), collect data on preferences and decide what to select (data and measurement), and design and execute the project (science and art). High school students can examine root causes of the refugee crisis (economics, geography, and history), propose solutions that demonstrate both nations' compassion and sovereign rights (civics), and call people to action (argumentative writing and art).

Instead of skimming the surface to arrive at an oversimplified solution, slower, in-depth study on a topic increases understanding. Immersed in ambiguity and uncertainty, the learners experience ideal conditions for learning. This condition can be brief or extended—either way, it primes the brain for engagement. This is why deeper, questing-type learning makes such a difference for the learner. He or she is building knowledge differently than before. In fact, we propose that questing, as a pedagogical framework, offers bigger, deeper, more authentic opportunities for students to build content knowledge all while being interested, engaged, and ready to receive the new learning.

### Active, Intentional Cycle

The second tenet is that the learner engages in an active, intentional cycle with clear goals and right-sized, actionable steps. The *extended cycle of expertise*, which is based on Carl Bereiter and Marlene Scardamalia's (1993) and James Paul Gee's (2007) work, is intentional and actionable because it has goals. Teachers can intentionally build the cycle of expertise, shown in figure 2.1, in an instructional sequence. Students need to be invested in a new problem that will require new learning. When they hit the frustration zone, the level of engagement and need to hit the next level help them persevere through the new learning. They learn and solidify new skills through repetition and multiple iterations of problem-solving pathways, leaving them with a feeling of accomplishment as they master the specific challenge at hand.

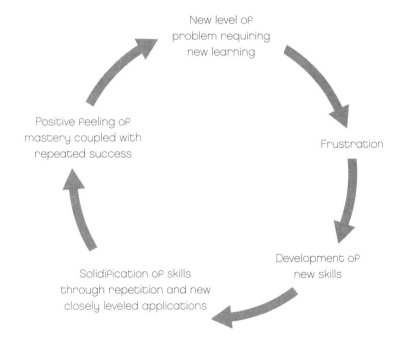

*Source: Adapted from Bereiter & Scardamalia, 1993, and Gee, 2007, as cited in Alcock, 2014.*

Figure 2.1: Extended cycle of expertise.

Each new challenging skill sends learners through this cycle. For example, an elementary school student might be given a mathematics problem with fractions. Because the student isn't familiar with fractions, he or she will have to learn new skills to solve, or master, the problem. Because the student doesn't yet have the required skills, he or she gets frustrated trying to solve the problem. With help, the student develops the skills he or she needs to solve fractions. Practice by way of repeating and applying the new skills in a carefully scaffolded manner helps the student solidify the required new skills. The student feels positive when he or she masters the skills and can repeatedly solve mathematical fraction problems. The student is willing and ready to try attaining more new skills. This results in the spiraling aspect of the extended cycle of expertise.

The extended cycle of expertise shows that the need for a sense of accomplishment (from positive feelings of mastery) couples with repeated success; it is that coupling that propels the momentum of learning toward the desire for cognitive challenge in a new problem or increased difficulty. The student needs this repeated success. Thus, a combination of appropriate-level challenge, timely feedback, and an observable growth in skill or knowledge creates a deeply satisfying learner experience. This extended cycle of expertise is an active cycle of clear goals (specific new skills) and right-sized (challenging but not impossible), actionable steps (presents specific goals).

Additionally, connecting the skills required to solve fractions to a meaningful quest means the learner is thinking deeply about the skills and concepts. When he or she masters the skills, the student, in effect, is an expert. Then the time is right for an increased challenge, a more difficult version of the fraction problem. When students experience frustration, their level of engagement and need to hit the next level of knowledge help them persevere through the new learning (Haskell, 2012). That tension propels students' learning.

Goal achievement ceases to be the point for this student. The learner learns how to learn: contending with frustration, having the courage to try, persevering, seeing the immediate results, and figuring out what to do next. The learner also grows an ability to self-regulate (monitoring how one is doing and feeling), self-evaluate (stepping back and judging current work), and self-motivate (setting learning goals and committing to how one will achieve them; Stiggins, 2017). This occurs, in part, through the formative assessment process chapter 8 (page 97) describes.

Questing leverages the extended cycle of expertise by requiring students and teachers to do the following nine steps during the tenet of engagement that invokes an active, intentional cycle.

1. Create and clarify the target (find a new problem or level).
2. Make an initial plan of action (experience frustration).
3. Experiment and try the initial plan (experience frustration).
4. Seek feedback and complete data collection (develop new skills).

5. Reflect by reading and processing the feedback (develop new skills).

6. Change or continue with the plan of action (solidify skills through repetition and closely leveled applications).

7. Change or continue experimenting (experience positive feeling from repeated success).

8. Adjust the target (find a new problem or level that requires new learning).

9. Repeat these steps.

As an example, in elementary schools around the world, students learn about life cycles of butterflies and other living creatures. Through the lens of the active, intentional cycle, that learning might look something like the following.

* **New problem level:** Learning launches with a question such as, What is the life cycle of an animal? or How does a caterpillar become a butterfly?

* **Frustration:** The answers to those questions are full of sophisticated concepts and domain-specific vocabulary such as *chrysalis*, *metamorphosis*, and *pupa*. To push through this, a teacher might engage several modalities of instruction, including oral explanation, text-based information, and symbolic representation.

* **Skill development and solidification:** The teacher continues working with multiple modalities, layering in observations, experiments, and real-world experience (hatching caterpillars in the classroom) that students observe. All the while, students are practicing—through oral explanations and written descriptions—all the scientific concepts and domain-specific words.

* **Positive feeling of mastery:** Through formative assessment and continued work, students move from receptive to expressive, from receiving and experiencing the information to owning and sharing it.

* **New problem level:** Armed with their new knowledge, students are ready for new learning.

The process is similar in middle or high school, except that students bring their background knowledge.

* **New problem level:** Learning launches with a question such as, How is a butterfly's life cycle similar to a frog's life cycle? What is happening inside the chrysalis at a cellular level? or How does their habitat affect the life cycle of different butterfly species?

* **Frustration:** Conceptual understanding from previous learning is essential knowledge here. Students now figure out how to find the answers to the questions, pushing beyond what is easy to acquire in an effort to discover the most meaningful, relevant information.

- ✳ **Skill development and solidification:** Again, teachers continue the work through multiple modalities, layering in observations, experiments, and opportunities for students to demonstrate what they are learning.
- ✳ **Positive feeling of mastery:** The process in secondary school is much like that at lower grade levels, with students not only explaining the new knowledge but masterfully weaving in all prior knowledge as an anchor for new concepts and vocabulary.
- ✳ **New problem level:** The cycle begins again with new problems, questions, or opportunities for investigations.

## Social, Collaborative Opportunities

Through this tenet, the learner engages in social, collaborative opportunities that grow expertise on a topic. The learning is shared not only between student and teacher but among everyone in the affinity space (which can include a meeting, an online discussion forum, or a playing field, among others). Students use networks like those described in chapter 5 (page 51) to build teams and create a kind of learning cooperative. They seek out physically close or virtual interactors. In addition to seeking feedback here, others in these spaces may view the student as an expert in some instances. For example, a student who creates a project in *Minecraft* and uploads it to YouTube has learned both content knowledge and peripheral skills around using *Minecraft* and screen capture technologies. As a result, other students who seek to replicate those actions might seek out this expert as one who can contribute to their learning processes.

Learners benefit cognitively from sharing their learning (Fawcett & Garton, 2005). We find that most learners also take solace in the fact that they are not in it alone; someone else is out there who has gone through this, or a similar journey, before. Whether someone guides the student through a particular challenge or offers guidance throughout the whole quest, he or she builds trust and rapport that can lead to future collaboration and supporting others who need assistance.

This space nurtures growth because of the many ways to participate and multiple routes to achieve status, all bound together by a common interest. For example, in John Hunter's *World Peace Game* (http://worldpeacegame.org), students strategize and navigate complex challenges to help save the world. Through this process, students learn via deep conversation and experience the extended cycle of expertise's frustration phase. Collectively, players examine alternate pathways to grow from that failure, increasing their problem-solving skills and abilities to ask higher-level-thinking questions (about strategy and resources). The comments sections on *Minecraft* YouTube videos are another example. They are replete with conversations and instructional videos between novices and experts—a perfect example of social, collaborative learning. In these kinds of spaces, novices try their skills. These affinity spaces are in stark comparison to classrooms, where students are at times afraid to ask questions or nervous to try something new. Questing helps foster technological and information literacy, which are crucial 21st century skills (Partnership for 21st Century Learning, n.d.).

The quest's goal is to have meaningful learning moments that grow expertise, not necessarily to produce experts in each quest. In fact, during a questing experience a learner may realize that he or she no longer enjoys the topic or field of study. This too can be very powerful learning, and the learning community can celebrate as deeply as when realizing a great passion and love for a topic.

## Design Options

The remainder of this chapter explores three design options that are helpful in designing contemporary questing experiences. For each option—(1) question design, (2) game design, and (3) network design—we will provide a brief overview as well as make explicit connections to the tenets of engagement. Whether you are dipping your toe in the water or are a burgeoning expert in inquiry, gaming, or networking in affinity spaces, you will guide students toward options that are right for them and for your classroom during a quest. Students can participate in one or all of these designs depending on the amount of time you have and your resource range (such as technology, games, off-site visits, and the like). We explore each design—question, game, and network—more fully in chapter 3 (page 25), chapter 4 (page 35), and chapter 5 (page 51).

### Question Design Choices

Regardless of topic or ultimate design decision, questions are necessary for all quests. Inquiry, which is the first learner engagement query and a design type, is the starting point for quests with game and network design. Inquiry leads to a quest because a learner must make choices that compel him or her to launch and navigate a quest. By nature, a learner is an inquirer, asking questions that require imagination, exploration, reexamination, and reworking.

Questions help merge emotionally gripping topics with learning targets such as the following Common Core State Standards for mathematics and for English language arts (National Governors Association Center for Best Practices [NGA] & Chief State School Officers [CCSSO], 2010b, 2010c).

* Write a meaningful argument (W.9–10.1).
* Write a helpful informational piece (W.11–12.2.a).
* Create charts to display data collected (3.MD.3).
* Identify whether there is a correlation in data and describe the relationship between two variables (HSS.ID.B.6).
* Design a model (HSG.MG.A.3).
* Create a character (W.3.3).
* Solve a problem with double-digit multiplication (4.NBT.B.5).

We introduce four distinct but interrelated types of questions here, discuss each at length in chapter 3 (page 25), and flesh them out in chapter 8 (page 97).

1. **Essential questions** promote inquiry in a topic, skill, or concept. The teacher designs these questions because the teacher knows what content and skills are most significant (and must be addressed) in the curriculum.

2. **Driving questions** guide research, action, and creation. Inspired by essential questions, students generate driving questions. These questions optimize student ownership, help students establish the challenge, and aid in their mapping out an approach to inquiry. With these, the learner engages with relevant, worthy inquiries and experiences that are interesting or emotionally gripping.

3. **Probing questions** deeply examine statements. Teachers can design these alone or co-create them with students to help examine assumptions based on evidence. Probing questions help students navigate learning goals and make sense of information or results.

4. **Reflection questions** encourage deep thinking about what the student learned and its impact on him or her. These questions help students during deliverable development, guiding revisions as well as monitoring how they feel about their process and progress.

Table 2.1 links the question types to the tenets of engagement.

**Table 2.1: Question Design Connections to Tenets of Engagement**

| Design Connections | Engagement Tenet |
|---|---|
| The teacher designs *essential* questions to begin a student's quest. The student drafts a series of *driving* questions to guide his or her inquiry process. | The learner engages with relevant, worthy inquiries and experiences that are interesting or emotionally gripping. |
| The teacher uses *probing* questions for the student to actively consider, guiding the extended cycle of expertise as the student develops patterns, solutions, prototypes, and creations. This may lead to new or nuanced driving questions. | The learner engages in an active, intentional cycle with clear goals and right-sized, actionable steps. |
| The student connects to others through a shared interest in specific questions, topics, or creation examination. As students share their thinking and development, *reflection* questions guide revisions. | The learner engages in social, collaborative opportunities that grow expertise. |

Chapter 3 focuses both on inquiry development and the spaces where learners can pursue those questions.

## Game Design Choices

Game design encourages students to learn while playing or designing a game. Neither learners nor teachers need to be fluent in the art of game design. Both can choose game design and its options without a background in game design. Good questing games are those that are challenging enough to be fun, but effectively teach content and skills so players do not quit when the game challenges them further. There is a balance between a task's challenge and the support provided to prepare players to accomplish that task or collection of tasks; that is known as reaching a *win state* (a phrase the gaming community employs to explain how to win any game that has more than one way to win). The same is true for quests—there is more than one way to move forward.

Different kinds of computer languages, such as Visual Basic, have evolved from BASIC. Visit Code.org (www.code.org) if you're interested in learning more. (Visit **go.Solution Tree.com/instruction** for live links to the websites mentioned in this book.) Chapter 4 (page 35) further explains game options, when learners make the following choices.

* The type of game that fits best for the desired learning: cooperative, competitive, or simulation
* Whether the learner will play a game to learn or design a game for other learners
* Which existing games, affinity spaces, and models can support the questing experience

Table 2.2 connects the tenets of engagement and the game design model.

**Table 2.2: Game Design Connections to Tenets of Engagement**

| Design Connections | Engagement Tenet |
|---|---|
| Games without a worthy question, problem, or identity lose the player's interest quickly. Something must compel the player to exert effort, persist, practice, and strategize. For example, in the Game of Life, how do my career and personal choices impact financial stability? Or in a cell virtual immersion game, what patterns or discoveries emerge as I isolate cellular structures? How can I use gravity to reach a portal faster? How does this process shape the study of diseases? | The learner engages with relevant, worthy inquiries and experiences that are interesting or emotionally gripping. |

continued ➡

| Design Connections | Engagement Tenet |
|---|---|
| People do not play games for very long that are too easy or too hard; the pieces are not right sized in those cases. Engaging games spiral the required skill development in close alignment with the challenge's difficulty until the player can do things he or she previously perceived as impossible—and gets the opportunity to experience the benefit of learning those skills by "winning" certain levels. The learner is intentionally participating in the extended cycle of expertise. (See chapter 4, page 35, and chapter 9, page 115, for more about spiraling skill development.) | The learner engages in an active, intentional cycle with clear goals and right-sized, actionable steps. |
| Many games either connect players directly to each other (thereby creating networks) or already have networks (forums or other affinity spaces). Whether the game is multiplayer or individual, there is a clear goal. A sense of competition drives the need to both seek out and share experiences. Even individual-player games such as *The Sims* have popular forums where players post challenges, discussions, inspired narratives, challenge solutions, and fan fiction (spin-off stories). More challenging games require informational guides, mentors, and teammates, and inevitably, with spiraling skill development, players grow expertise. | The learner engages in social, collaborative opportunities that grow expertise. |

## Network Design Choices

Network design choices impact how learners will interact with peers, mentors, and topic experts. During that collaboration, they work together on questions or problems. For example, the network can involve talking with other people online or meeting face-to-face. Affinity spaces are a type of network.

The network design choices may feel natural to digital natives, who come to school equipped with strategies for connecting online, or *virtually*, with other people. However, our experience is that they may not be negotiating all these connections in meaningful or authentic ways. A network's power to support learning directly relates to the network's quality. During a quest of network design, students learn to navigate increasingly sophisticated spaces as they alternate between consuming content and producing and evaluating it ethically, safely, and efficiently.

Network design elements invite new perspectives as well as an opportunity to develop essential 21st century skills like technological and media literacy (Costa & Kallick, 2000; Jacobs & Alcock, 2017; Partnership for 21st Century Learning, n.d.). Chapter 5 (page 51) explains network design options, or *spaces*, in detail, with explanations for physical, plus, public, member, and mentor spaces. Table 2.3 explicitly connects the tenets of engagement with network design and its spaces.

**Table 2.3: Network Design Connections to Tenets of Engagement**

| Design Connections | Engagement Tenet |
|---|---|
| When exploring different network spaces, the student invites increasingly sophisticated resources—online forums, blogs, wikis, LISTSERVs, YouTube channels, field experts—into his or her learning. These collaborations help keep quests interesting and provide opportunities for discovering compelling resources. | The learner engages with relevant, worthy inquiries and experiences that are interesting or emotionally gripping. |
| Networking can be as simple as asking a nearby classmate a question or as complex as using computers to engage field leaders in conversation in real time. The communication is intentional, and its best effect occurs when the learner has a clear goal in mind. The student can make right-sized steps by starting with simple questions (like, "May I ask you a question?") and then broadening his or her scope. | The learner engages in an active, intentional cycle with clear goals and right-sized, actionable steps. |
| Collaborating with partners in small and large groups, plugging into and participating in physical and virtual networks, sharing ideas, making sense of questions, developing a solution, and offering insight about obstacles are all inherently social ways to grow expertise. | The learner engages in social, collaborative opportunities that grow expertise. |

Table 2.4 explains the connections between the tenets of engagement and some possible student responses through our disease example thread.

**Table 2.4: Disease Example Quest Connections to Tenets of Engagement**

| Tenet of Engagement Connection | Possible Student Questions and Responses |
|---|---|
| • Relevant<br>• Worthy<br>• Interesting | • How can my community be healthier?<br>• How can my community prevent the spread of infectious disease?<br>• How can I help my community be as healthy as possible? |

continued ➤

| Tenet of Engagement Connection | Possible Student Questions and Responses |
|---|---|
| • Active<br>• Intentionally cyclical<br>• Goal oriented | • There is a game I can play that is fun and engaging to help me learn more about my topic. Other people around the world play this game so I can see how I compare.<br>• I can use the information from this experience to affirm or refute information in a public resource that another state offers.<br>• I can learn about writing an effective informational.<br>• I can reach out to a professional organization, such as the Centers for Disease Control and Prevention (CDC).<br>• I can reach out to a museum about my topic.<br>• I can participate in the affinity space from the CDC about diseases.<br>• I can fact-check information. I can synthesize information from multiple sources. |
| • Social<br>• Collaborative<br>• Proficient | • We can provide feedback to the public resource to make it more accurate for their community.<br>• We can create our own version of the resource for my local community. |

## Coda

This chapter introduced you to the tenets of engagement and how the three quest lenses—question design, game design, and network design—support those tenets. Quests are loaded with attention-grabbing moments that spark relevant, worthy inquiries; active, intentional cycles that result in wrong turns, feedback, reiterations, and finally expertise; and an abundance of social, collaborative opportunities. The next three chapters invite you to begin using questing as an instructional framework using one or a combination of these three lenses. You can use them in the classroom for any quest.

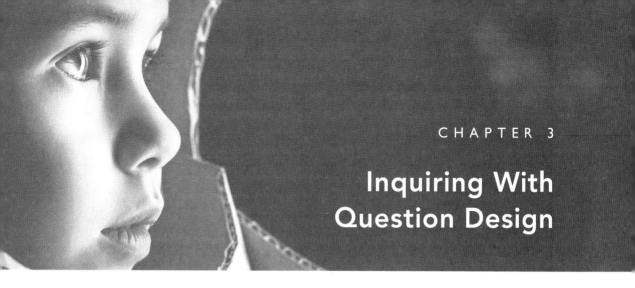

# Inquiring With Question Design

Questioning is at the heart of the first tenet of engagement, in which the learner engages with relevant, worthy inquiries and experiences that are interesting or emotionally gripping. Students need to learn how to ask relevant, critical questions to make sense of varied and often contradictory information. Developing a deeper understanding of key concepts and processes can help them flourish in an unpredictable world (Partnership for 21st Century Learning, n.d.).

Yet inquiry is *not* a spectator sport or for the faint of heart. It requires active participation. This pursuit asks the learner to tap into executive functioning skills such as judgment, synthesis, and prioritization (Willis, 2011, 2016). During quests, students can immerse themselves in exploration, and teachers can engage them with different types of questions to help them learn not only about their challenge topic but also how to *form* questions. Regardless of where or when the learning takes place, students can learn to challenge assumptions with different question types, articulate existing tensions, or generate an idea by design. Instructional guidance helps students to this point. The disease sample questing thread shows question design in action.

## Question Types

The following sections focus on the question types introduced in chapter 2 (page 13): (1) essential questions, (2) driving questions, (3) probing questions, and (4) reflection questions. We explain how that connects to curriculum standards and student agency to pose, navigate, and pursue those questions. How teachers handle questions determines whether students move from apprentices to experts, from dependent learners to independent problem solvers. In the questing framework, a teacher pays closer attention to and cultivates students' capacity to raise and examine their own questions.

### Essential Questions

The teacher designs essential questions to promote genuine inquiry in the topic, skill, or concept. Jay McTighe and Grant Wiggins (2013) advocate "provocative and generative" essential questions: "By tackling such questions, learners are engaged in *uncovering* the depth and richness of a topic that might otherwise be obscured by simply *covering* it" (p. 3).

Essential questions in different subject areas might sound like the following.

* **English language arts:** What is my purpose for reading? How does it influence how I read?
* **History:** How does trade connect people? How does trade create conflict?
* **Mathematics:** What changes have occurred here (rate, transformation, or equation) and why?
* **Physical education:** How do I kick the ball to get it where I want it to go? How do I improve my hand-eye coordination?
* **Social studies:** What communities am I part of? How do I help each community I am part of? What is my role as a citizen of this community? How and when do we protect against persecution or discrimination?
* **Science:** How does the body work to repair itself? Can I help promote that repair?

You will leverage your own content expertise, knowledge about time parameters, and understanding of students' sophistication level to develop questions that are accessible, intriguing, transferrable (to a range of topics, challenges, or texts), and centered on big ideas. These overarching questions develop ideas, trigger conversations, and present resources that can generate related questions in students.

## Driving Questions

The student develops driving questions. Typically, the questions evolve over time. The journey often starts off with a generic, broad question and becomes more nuanced and complex as students drill down. Driving questions often launch from the essential question as in the following examples. The arrows in the following examples show a student's potential progression through driving inquiries.

* **World languages:** Inspired by the essential question, How do cultural artifacts and practices reveal a people's beliefs and values? → What is the Day of the Dead about? → How does it compare to Halloween? → Why is it important to the Mexican people?
* **English language arts:** Inspired by the essential question, How do I grab my audience's attention and make it care about what I say? → What am I trying to say? → Does it make sense to me? → Will it make sense to others? → How do I know when I'm finished?
* **Science:** Inspired by the essential question, How do living things get energy? → What is photosynthesis? → How does photosynthesis work? → How do plants get energy from the sun in places where it rains a lot of the time? → Do plants look different in places that are dry and sunny versus in places where it rains a lot?

*   **History:** Inspired by the essential question, What caused the U.S. Civil War? → Was the Civil War only about slavery? → What was the war's legacy? → Whom did it really help, and whom did it hurt? → How has the United States progressed as a nation? → What core issues today in the United States show that the battle for equality continues?
*   **Mathematics:** Inspired by the essential question, What is fair, and how can mathematics help us understand that question? → What is fair in this situation? → What rules can I use to quantify or calculate fairness? → How do I show my thinking? → To what extent is one way of calculating fairness unfair to others?

Students may already be raising questions like these, but typically are not acting on them. Continuing to provide opportunities for them to create driving questions can be a lovely transition into the questing framework.

## Probing Questions

Probing questions necessitate the awareness and self-confidence to articulate what the learner doesn't know. These questions can challenge what learners know to be true ("I thought it was the other way"); take them to unexpected places ("I hadn't considered that"); or make them feel anxious ("I have a deadline"), impatient ("This is taking so long"), or aggravated ("This isn't what I learned before"). But even when the question feels difficult or uncertain, the possibility of what it can lead to captures enough of a student's attention and imagination to propel him or her forward in the extended cycle of expertise.

The teacher *and* students design probing questions to reveal insights; examine more deeply; and consider alternate ways of seeing information, ideas, or design. They are not specific to a topic's or skill's essential question, but rather grow a learner's mindset. They can be subject specific or anchored to skills that are prevalent across subjects. Here are a few examples.

*   What is the evidence to support your idea, claim, conclusion, or inference?
*   How does _____ depend on _____?
*   Is there another way of looking at this?
*   What is the pattern here? What does it help you see?
*   What happens when the rules change?

Be mindful of the second learner engagement tenet, which says the learner engages in an active, intentional cycle with clear goals and right-sized, actionable steps. Child psychologist Alison Gopnik warns that "when we start teaching too much, too soon, we're inadvertently cutting off paths of inquiry and exploration that kids might otherwise pursue on their own" (as cited in Berger, 2014, p. 43). Beware that pitfall and of using leading probing questions. Teaching too much too soon diminishes the challenge's complexity.

### Reflection Questions

Reflection questions typically come from the teacher to guide the student as he or she refines and revises driving and probing questions, research sources, and deliverables. Sometimes, students ask themselves reflection questions so they can answer outstanding questions. They help the student continue to reflect on the quality of the work (in relation to curriculum expectations) as well as the experience (in relation to process). Students use reflection inquiries to continue refining, revising, or reimagining a deliverable. Some examples follow.

* How do you continue to revise your writing to say what you mean?
* What are you focusing on as you perform this piece? How does that affect your performance quality?
* What does it mean? What is the best way to explain it? Does your answer or solution make sense?

Reflection questions help keep learners on track and develop habits for refinement and revision while the quest is ongoing (Costa & Kallick, 2000; Kallick & Zmuda, 2017a). Because a quest enables smaller learning scenarios that lead to the destination, reflecting on and revising those parts support ongoing success during the quest.

## Instructional Guidance

Although questing tends to be open ended, outlining some guidance helps facilitate the kind of culture that results in questions that require higher-order-thinking skills.

* **Mind your body language:** Avoid body language and comments that may send a message that a student's line of inquiry is not helpful, desirable, or appropriate. Make space for students to pursue fledgling curiosities by welcoming questions even when they are uncomfortable or exhausting.
* **Co-create criteria for questions:** You and your students agree on these criteria as a class before quests begin. Make sure you and your students phrase the criteria in accessible language, as in table 3.1, with a tenet aspect preceding them.
* **Clarify roles:** An inquiry-designed quest means posing and pursuing questions to navigate through unknown territory. The beginning of that journey might feel disorienting. Students need to experience this; saving them from this struggle (even if they really want assistance) limits their opportunities to grow. In this space, it is helpful to clarify the teacher's and students' roles.

  In your role as teacher, you provide students the following things.
  * Provide enough time and space to generate lots of questions (about an essential question, a topic focus statement, or a text).
  * Teach the difference between open and closed questions.

**Table 3.1: Possible Student Question Criteria**

| Criteria for What Students Should Ask Themselves | Tenet of Engagement Connection |
|---|---|
| The question means something to me. I find both the idea and how the question is framed motivating and inspiring. | • Relevant<br>• Worthy<br>• Interesting |
| The more I make sense of the question, the more interesting it becomes. The question has momentum. My question leads to more questions. | • Active<br>• Intentionally cyclical<br>• Goal oriented |
| I want to share my ideas, creations, and conclusions with others. Their feedback helps me refine my thinking and next steps. I can provide feedback to those who are stuck or need another perspective. | • Social<br>• Collaborative<br>• Proficient |

*Source: © Alcock, Fisher, & Zmuda, 2015.*

- ★ Model and encourage how to capture the evolution of questions (using a graphic organizer, for example).
- ★ Observe rather than interject.

A student's role requires the following.

- ★ Brainstorm and write questions as others say them; make no judgments.
- ★ Accept awkward pauses and uncomfortable stretches of silence. That means that students have space to explore fresh thinking (Rowe, 1987; Swift & Gooding, 1983).
- ★ Prioritize questions based on whether they are open (diverse approaches, multiple perspectives, and multiple possible solutions) or closed (one right answer), the areas of interest they address, and their actionability (the ability to pursue one based on resource and time accessibility).
- ★ Push your assumptions and ideas through research, conversation, and reflection.

- ★ **Model powerful, actionable questions:** Identify illustrative questions that come from a variety of sources that you and students can collect. Examples of these powerful, actionable questions include the following.
  - ★ What makes something funny?
  - ★ Why aren't there any more dinosaurs?
  - ★ How much will college cost when you go to school? Is it worth the investment?
- ★ **Implement reflection time:** John Dewey (1916) coined the aphorism, "We do not learn from experience, we learn from reflecting on experience" (p. 78).

One of inquiry's broader aims is to learn more about one's dispositions, attitudes, and feelings when experiencing the pursuit. Work with students to identify a handful of questions, like those that follow, on which students can regularly reflect to guide their next experience. The responses to these questions can shape the next iteration of a design, clarify the next step, identify another significant goal, or engender another quest.

- ★ What process did you go through to pursue this inquiry? What problems did you encounter along the way? How did you solve them?
- ★ What did you learn about yourself as you worked on this piece?
- ★ As you look at the result of your inquiry, what's one thing that you would like to improve on?
- ★ What were your standards for this inquiry experience? How did you measure up?

## Sample Questing Thread

Throughout the remainder of this book, chapters will visit the questing thread of disease to provide a common illustrative example for elementary, middle, and high school. As a topic, disease has range because it connects to biology, chemistry, history, current events, mathematics, literature, and innovation. It also connects to emotions, including fear, empathy, and anger.

Table 3.2 lays out the four types of questions with disease as the focal point.

**Table 3.2: Inquiry Types by Disease Questing Thread**

| Questing Thread: Disease | Who Is Asking | Inquiry Type |
|---|---|---|
| • The elementary school question is, How can we stop spreading germs? The middle or high school question is, How do we prevent the spread of deadly diseases?<br>• At what cost? (Note that *cost* purposefully has multiple meanings—financial expenses, quarantines, and public panic, for instance.) | Teacher asks student | Essential |
| • What is the evidence to support your conclusion, decision, or solution?<br>• Is there another way of looking at this?<br>• What is the pattern here? What does it help you see?<br>• What sort of impact do you think _____?<br>• How do you think people feel based on what is happening? How does it impact their actions?<br>• What do you feel is right?<br>• How might your assumptions about _____ influence your thinking about _____? | Student and teacher ask each other | Probing |

| Questing Thread: Disease | Who Is Asking | Inquiry Type |
|---|---|---|
| • Where did this disease come from? Why now? Can we eradicate it?<br>• How does it travel? How do people catch it?<br>• What are the symptoms? How do we diagnose it?<br>• How do we control, treat, or cure it? | Student asks him- or herself and affinity space members | Driving |
| • Does my conclusion make sense?<br>• What is the best way to explain it? | Teacher asks student or student asks self | Reflection |

*Visit **go.SolutionTree.com/instruction** for a free reproducible version of this table.*

As students orient themselves in their explorations of diseases, you want them to actively examine and uncover questions to gather knowledge, synthesize diverse resources, and generate ideas for sharing. The following elementary, middle, and high school sections give scripts to help shape quests and encourage teachers to envision possibilities for question design at different grade levels.

## Elementary School

Elementary schools typically focus on healthy behaviors to avoid the spread of germs—washing hands before and after eating, washing hands after using the bathroom, and covering one's nose and mouth when sneezing or coughing. These habits are especially important to establish as cold and flu season approaches, as it has a significant impact on school attendance. How does a teacher get students to not only learn the habits but also see their importance? Teachers or students can generate quest ideas, but the student owns the quest. The point is the pursuit, not the origination.

Let's start with the essential question, How can we stop the spread of germs? The teacher can describe what a germ is and then pour whole-wheat flour on a plate to represent germs. Have three or four students come up and press their hands in the flour. Then, give the class playtime to build with blocks. After a few minutes, gather the class together to show how germs spread based on the number of blocks where flour appears.

The teacher asks students a follow-up question, "What could have been done to stop the spread of flour or germs?"

One student might say, "Wash your hands." Another student might ask, "How am I supposed to wash my hands?" Another student might say he heard that singing "Three Blind Mice" as you rinse off is a good idea. The teacher probes, "Why is that a good idea?" Another student might pipe up that she doesn't like using hot water because it burns her hands and say, "Is it OK to just use cold water? Will that help stop the germs?" Another student might ask, "Can we make signs so that we can remember what to do even when a teacher isn't there?" Another student can offer, "Where else can germs live? Can we wash other things besides our hands?" Already, the learning experience has hooked students in the importance and messiness of stopping germs from spreading. Students generate compelling questions and offer tentative ideas as to how to help, reflecting the engagement tenet that has the learner engaging with relevant, worthy inquiries and experiences that are interesting or emotionally gripping.

The teacher can then engage students in probing questions to uncover more information about their own questions. Do read-alouds using books that offer good information. To start students on their way to taking action by making signs, work with the students to help change the words to a familiar song (perhaps to "Three Blind Mice," or whatever the students suggest).

Students may draw or locate illustrations to create a how-to sequence of what to do when washing hands. Have students engage in role play set in a doctor's office or at family mealtime. These collaborative learning experiences relate to the engagement tenet that has students collaborating; here, they articulate and test helpful steps based on their readings. They focus on basic informational writing, speaking, and revising their directions based on feedback from teacher and peers.

To honor the student who wants to wash other objects besides hands, students may ask, "What can dry after being washed in soap and water? What would be ruined if that happened?" During this inquiry, a new question might pop up: "Are there other ways of cleaning something?" The teacher guides students back to the essential question, reminding them that they are learning how to prevent the spread of germs, and asks the probing question, "If something is clean, does that mean it has no germs?"

## Middle School

As we play out a middle school scenario, let's return to the essential question to launch a multidisciplinary journey: How do we prevent the spread of deadly diseases? At what cost? The teacher may hook students in a variety of ways to create a compassionate and serious atmosphere. A few examples follow.

* **Anonymously survey students about what diseases they worry about due to a personal connection or something that appeared in the news headlines:** Students may begin to ask driving questions such as, "How can I find accurate information about a disease that someone I love has? What rights do I have to talk to medical professionals (as a patient or as a patient's family member)? When does knowing more actually hurt me or the patient?"

* **Share the story of an artist, Mary Beth Heffernan, as she read about the Ebola virus and health workers who wore protective gear:** She asked herself, "What would it be like to be a patient? What would it be like to not see a person's face for days on end?" And she developed a solution (http://n.pr /2xlPiJs). Students may begin to ask driving questions such as, "How can we help patients feel better? What can patients safely receive for their disease? What organizations provide for patients and their families?"

* **Evaluate data about pneumonia, a deadly disease that impacts young children especially:** Students may begin to ask driving questions such as, "What is the deadliest disease right now? How widespread is it? To what extent is it under control?" Another thread might be a historical one that spurs students to ask questions like, "What is the deadliest disease of all time? Who did it impact? If it was cured, how?"

Students could pursue, in multiple subjects, the compelling questions they generate. Based on the initial hook's design and related questions, students could engage in data analysis, historical research, public health policy, pharmaceutical innovations, service learning projects, or visual art as a public service announcement.

## High School

For high school, let's take a look at ideas that students might come up with based on their personal connections and initial research. Subject areas in play are in parentheses. Students can research a disease of their choosing and then engage in one of the following.

* **Design a public health message (using media or forms that students are comfortable with) to relay key information and reveal misinformation:** They may ask driving questions such as, "To what extent do people have good information about what they need to prevent, minimize exposure to, or treat the disease? How can I help verify and communicate public health messages based on valid scientific information?" (English language arts, world languages, health, arts, and science are applicable subject areas.)
* **Trace a given disease's origin and spread to describe its extent and when it could potentially reach epidemic status:** They may ask driving questions such as, "What is this disease? What are the symptoms? What is the prognosis? What causes it to spread? When does it become a global health concern?" (English language arts, world languages, health, world history, and science are applicable subject areas.)
* **Identify promising new treatments for a given disease and how they can cure the disease or make it manageable:** An example is how type 1 diabetes patients receive healthy pancreatic cells from deceased donors to be able to produce insulin (National Institute of Diabetes and Digestive and Kidney Diseases, 2013). Focus on both the benefits and the potential risks (*costs* per the essential question) of a new treatment. They may ask driving questions such as, "How does this disease affect people? Is a cure or vaccine possible? What are the major challenges medical professions are working on to combat the disease? What is the government doing—or not doing—to help?" (Ethics, health, and science are applicable subject areas.)

## Coda

This chapter focused on question types that may be familiar to many, but empowering students to actively question is a viable and worthy goal. Age and expertise do not limit one's capacity to question; students are perfectly capable of framing questions to push deeper into the content, make sense of the challenge in front of them, and develop aspirations. Valuing inquiry means finding the space to question *with* students instead of *for* them. Teaching students how to use various question types and encouraging student-driven questions can help turn receiving information into actionable pursuits.

# CHAPTER 4

# Playing With Game Design

Questing is a way to help exercise and increase *gaming literacy*, which is the ability to look at the world through the lens of game design to create specific kinds of meanings; educational researcher Eric Zimmerman (2011) also contends that gaming literacy "stand[s] for a new set of cognitive, creative, and social skills" (p. 25). This literacy helps a game designer not only make a good game but also help solve real-world problems.

This chapter explores game design as a questing option, which includes both creating and playing games as choices. We focus on the key steps in game design for learning, as well as the art of using good games to maximize learning experiences. All kinds of games—card, board, dice, video, tabletop, and live-action role play—can be effective. The more you know about them, the more easily you can re-create play in the classroom and promote gaming literacy development.

This chapter also explores how games captivate players and goes into the research explaining why games are such effective learning tools. Various sections tackle different game types—cooperative, competitive, simulation, and combination—and how to design or select the most appropriate one given the topic, the experience students desire, the quest you want to help create, and the curriculum standards. Finally, we revisit the disease example's questing thread to describe how game design allows students to simulate challenges and revise their paths.

## Extended Cycle of Expertise in Games

When they choose game options for questing, students take a worthy problem and pair it with play. When players begin a new game, there is no expectation that they will master the game the first time they play it. They try, and when they fail, they learn not to do that action. Then they try a different approach. This trial and error is a natural part of the learning process (as evidenced by the extended cycle of expertise) and a key element for understanding why game design theory in classroom instruction is so engaging.

As students play or design games, they learn about their quest challenge. There is actual game play (where the content knowledge and practiced skills are the target), interaction about a game in an affinity space (where a product like an argumentative essay about the game is the deliverable), or game design (where creating the narrative, rules, and cycle of expertise for a player to experience is the deliverable).

There is no one right way to find the win state, which in game design means to accomplish a task. Win states are subjective, depending on the learner's perspective, the elements, the teacher's agreement, and even the contributing affinity spaces. You can win as a teacher by eliciting deeper commitments from students to their learning, which presents as engagement and higher short-term and long-term learning target mastery levels. For students, win states might be milestones they have met or mastered or their quest's completion. Students may see the win as an elevated status, where they have become trusted professionals (in affinity spaces, for instance).

All the win states, big or small, matter because they represent active learning. When playing or designing games, students gain experience by participating in an event that causes them to make choices, deal with consequences, and move forward. Only the learning target's or goal's size is different; it can align to any set of standards or curriculum non-negotiables you share with the learner. The steps to improve might be right-sized learning targets, such as adding single-digit numbers or multiplying within ten as players gain resources. As game difficulty increases, the required skills grow more sophisticated. For example, players may need to mentally complete addition and multiplication to quickly make choices during a game.

Learners can discover principles on their own and construct knowledge or practice skills by working through real-world problems or quality questions. In fact, video game designer Will Wright (2007), who created *The Sims* and *Spore*, compares his games to Montessori toys. Both involve perceiving patterns and relationships through cycles of action, observation, and feedback. He designed the cycle of expertise into his games, and reports thinking of them as well-crafted learning experiences to provide a new lens for seeing the world. Video games in particular can help students and educators realize the sound educational learning theories of Maria Montessori, David A. Kolb, and John Dewey, who promote a learner's free exploration within a given framework or structure (as cited in Squire, 2011).

The ways to interact with games and the topics that are the basis for that interaction are different depending on the students. For elementary students, touch technologies like trackpads and touch devices like smartphones and some laptops satisfy the same learning process. Elementary students generally interact with video games to learn concepts like the alphabet, rhythm, and colors. Middle and high school students can use *simulators*, or games that mimic experiences or skills, to learn complex skill sets like world languages, dating, anti-bullying, and heart surgery basics. The art of game design can maximize learning about systems design, storytelling, art, music, applied mathematics (for scores and resources), logistics (for rules and balance of play), any content area or subject matter, characters, setting, and plot, as well as collaboration with peers, social interactions as a part of game play, identity development, and project management—just for starters.

# Game Types

Cooperative and competitive games are inherently social, and many games offer internal networks where players can chat, problem solve, and strategize. BoardGameGeek (https://boardgamegeek.com) offers new game announcements, reviews, and popular affinity spaces for all kinds of games. (Visit **go.SolutionTree.com/instruction** to access live links to the websites mentioned in this book.) Designing a game requires collaboration with the intended audience in search of feedback and within the team creating the game. In turn, the designer incorporates the feedback into new iterations of the game, and ensures that the game gives the player feedback.

Whether they are playing or designing, students who quest via game design have three basic game types, plus combinations, from which they can choose: (1) cooperative, (2) competitive, and (3) simulation. The following sections explore each game type in detail.

## Cooperative Games

Cooperative games require players to work together, an element that emphasizes the third learner engagement tenet. Many players prefer this type because they create connections rather than feelings of hostility or betrayal, which competition can cause. Communication and collaboration, including anti-bullying and peacemaking skills, are the 21st century skills students will nourish during cooperative game play (Partnership for 21st Century Learning, n.d.). The motivation to play comes from the thrill of collaboration with a team to do something bigger than anything a single player might be able to do.

Players may work with roles, skills, or content to reach a win state as a team; getting there requires each member's contributions. Often, players cannot win cooperative games if any one player prioritizes personal success over that of the team. Consider games like *Castle Panic*, *World Peace Game*, *Minecraft*, and *Spaceteam* to pose survival challenges to groups. See table 4.1 for more examples of cooperative games.

**Table 4.1: Cooperative Games**

| Content Area or Skill | Game | Description |
|---|---|---|
| Sequencing and memory | *Hanabi* | Students will create a firework display by citing details from cards that everyone needs but only one player knows. |

continued ➡

| Content Area or Skill | Game | Description |
|---|---|---|
| Problem solving | *Forbidden Island* | Students will rescue one another using problem solving and a jigsaw puzzle of the character's skills. |
| History | *Freedom: The Underground Railroad* | Students will coordinate and raise funds to help runaway slaves achieve freedom. |
| Literacy | *Lord of the Rings* board games | Students will play story characters and cooperate to win. |

## Competitive Games

During competitive games, players try to reach a win state before the other players or against a scenario, adventure, or computer artificial intelligence (AI). The motivation to play comes from competition. Chess, *Monopoly*, and *Risk* are examples of competitive board games, while games like *Garden Defense* and *Plants vs. Zombies* are examples of competitive tower defense computer games. *Counter-Strike, Dota 2, StarCraft: Brood War*, and *League of Legends* are competitive games in which *eSports* (competitive video gaming) and global tournaments offer millions of dollars to the professional players and teams. Often, these games create conditions to overcome, including resource management, or problems to solve, including puzzles or races. See table 4.2 for more examples of competitive games.

### Table 4.2: Competitive Games

| Content Area or Skill | Game | Description |
|---|---|---|
| Critical thinking | *Overwatch* | Students will play unique roles in teamed tournaments. |
| Literacy | *Dominion* | Students will play this game (with cards or online) to learn vocabulary and practice reading fluently. |
| Critical thinking, decision making, complex systems | *StarCraft II: Legacy of the Void* | Students will play this real-time strategy game around university courses, exploring everything from theory to calculus. |
| History, literacy, decision making | *7 Wonders, Amun-Re, Castles, Diplomacy, The Princes of Florence* | Students will play board games that require critical thinking. |

Teachers have used competitive games in classroom settings with mixed results (Nebel, Schneider, & Rey, 2016). In some cases, the affirmation they sense in their own abilities when they beat their classmates motivates students (Posselt & Lipson, 2016). However, students may shut down or reject a game because they don't often (or ever) win or they feel as if they are not equal to their competitors. We suggest avoiding competitive games in favor of cooperative or simulation games until students develop enough proficiency to enjoy competition.

Consider using a competitive game that includes features such as tutorials or an artificial intelligence opponent to support students. Have students compete with the computer's artificial intelligence or their own personal best before competing with other students. When students do play a competitive game, it helps to include the work of Marzano (2010), where he outlines four ways to promote healthy competition.

1.  Provide inconsequential competition so the results do not negatively impact a student's grade.
2.  Connect to the curriculum's essential content and skills.
3.  Allow students to reflect and discuss the game rather than just add up the points and declare the winner.
4.  Provide students time to revise their notes or materials based on the game experience.

The point is to connect the game's fun and engaging experience to the learning and allow students to document and retain the new content knowledge or skills immediately following the game.

## Simulation Games

Simulation games can help learners develop a complex skill, such as a new language. During simulation games, players engage with a rehearsal or controlled practice of a given skill. The motivation to play comes from honing skills and solving problems within the simulation's safety. The goal is to achieve a personal best, achieve a skill set certification, or hold a record.

The Xbox Kinect and apps that utilize Google Cardboard are examples. Kinect effectively lets a player become the controller, and Google Cardboard is a virtual reality viewer that uses apps to do things like let players walk down a street in Paris and use their emerging French language skills to interact with people. Both allow for more immersive experiences than previous video games or simulations could offer. Table 4.3 (page 40) offers more simulation games.

**Table 4.3: Simulation Games**

| Content Area or Skill | Game | Description |
|---|---|---|
| Communication | *Emily Is Away* | Students will simulate dating and honesty in online chatting during this one-player game. |
| History | *Life Is Feudal: Forest Village* | Students will build a city and manage resources to simulate feudalism. |
| Perseverance | *Job Simulator* | Students will learn what it is like, in this single-player game, to have a job in a world where robots have taken over. |
| Anatomy, health | *Surgeon Simulator 2013* | Students will attempt life-saving surgery in this single-player game via graphic anatomy and body systems. |

Simulation games cover a rich range of experiences, such as space shuttle flight, submarine voyage, and driving. Some are strategy games, like *Sim City*, *FarmVille*, and *Spore*. Some are adventure or survival games, such as *Elite Dangerous* and *No Man's Sky*, which create a complete galaxy in which to explore and operate as a space trader. *Elite Dangerous* offers realistic in-game physics, and the spacecraft's complexity is challenging. The game requires mathematics to calculate faster-than-light and sublight speeds, with the player having to take into account things like slowing down before being pulled by a star's gravity.

## Combination Games

All three game types can intertwine with one another, either between games or within one game. For example, *Clash of Clans* uses competition, cooperation, and simulation. In the beginning, the game only allows play against artificial intelligence. The game heavily guides each move in a tutorial so the player succeeds despite knowing little about how to play. A simulation area lets players compete against AI skill-building levels, teaching different techniques. This is analogous to simulations that a pilot might go through before actually flying a plane. In the simulation, the prospective pilot receives opportunities to respond to different scenarios and practice his or her response to those scenarios. When the pilot is in the real plane, he or she will know how to respond to rapidly changing conditions. The player simultaneously competes against a player who has a similar skill level. After the player meets some game goals, the game releases the player to enter a clan of other players. In this clan, they bond socially, support one another, and compete against other clans. Other games with similar range and scope include *Minecraft* and *3DGameLab*.

The *3DGameLab* provides a structure in which teachers can design skill-building quests or tasks for the curriculum. This allows students to work through the required content knowledge and skills at their own pace and even give feedback about the quality of the experiences for the teacher to use to refine the curriculum. Students have opportunities to earn badges for skills, level up, gain experience points, and monitor progress toward the larger goal through the structure. They can also build larger quests or document their own questing in a tool that provides a structure, like the *3DGameLab*. These tools make questing easier in the classroom. However, they are not required.

## Game Design Choices

Just like any instructional framework, questing for learning requires preparation on your part. Be certain that your classroom, school, or district can support the options that interest students. Proactively seeking these options helps you provide limits and structures. Consider the following when extending quests with game design. If the student is the designer, he or she would consider the questions on page 43.

The subsequent sections help you do the following.

* Identify a best-fit game.
* Help students decide whether to play to learn or create to learn.
* Search for affinity spaces.

### Identify a Best-Fit Game

Some games work well for some students, but not for others. Vet options based on important considerations such as desired learning goals, available resources, and student readiness. Search for well-designed games, which provide information just when players need it and epitomize the extended cycle of expertise. They often do this with *tutorials*, *training grounds*, *sandboxes*, or *scrimmages*—simplified versions. The tutorial for *Clash of Clans* offers a giant yellow arrow that indicates what the player should do.

Other games, like *Minecraft*, feature a creative mode in which a player can practice with unlimited resources. In that game, the sandbox is the heart of how teachers use *Minecraft* as an education tool to teach any number of content areas and skills. Entire classrooms have moved into the sandbox space. (Search online for "*Minecraft* in education," "*Minecraft* and math literacy," "*Minecraft* and history," and so on to find examples of how teachers use the game in their classrooms.)

Then there are complex games. Again, consider learning goals and student readiness when determining best fit, but for complex games, also consider a student's need for incremental wins or small achievements. For example, in the board game *Puerto Rico*, the game can end when there are no more colonists, no more victory points, or no more spaces to fill. The existence of more than one way to win makes the game more complex and makes possible small achievements; difficult curriculum content or higher-order-thinking skills are suited for complex games.

The Entertainment Software Rating Board (www.esrb.org) gives some of the games we mention in this book a *mature* rating, meaning they're inappropriate for anyone under age seventeen. It is logical for elementary students and teachers to play E-rated (appropriate for everyone) video games, family board games, and basic card games in safe or limited-access affinity spaces.

## Help Students Decide to Play to Learn or Create to Learn

Questing via game design can mean playing to learn or creating to learn.

### Play to Learn

If they want to play to learn, students find *off-the-shelf* games, such as *Scrabble*, chess, and *Candy Crush Saga*—existing games. Table 4.4 offers more off-the-shelf games for players.

**Table 4.4: Off-the-Shelf Games**

| Content Area or Skill | Game | Description |
|---|---|---|
| Grammar, vocabulary | *Apples to Apples* | In this competitive card game, students will choose a word that describes another word. |
| Spelling, vocabulary | *WordXChange* | Students will create words and steal others' words by adding letters. |
| Problem solving, perseverance | All versions of *The Legend of Zelda* | Students will role play and solve puzzles in this single-player game. |
| Inferencing | *Dixit* | Students will practice storytelling, sentence crafting, and inferring in this competitive card game. |
| Narrative writing | *Everything* | Students will write a story from the perspective of any character (over one thousand are available). |
| Narrative writing | *Persona 5* | Students will write an alternate ending or a piece of fan fiction. |
| Argumentative writing | *Super Mario Kart* | Students will design a strategy and suggest why it is the best, fastest, most elegant, accurate way to reach a win state using a specific race. |
| Informational writing | *The Legend of Zelda: Breath of the Wild* | Students will write a description of how to solve challenges. |
| Data analysis | Any five games | Students will select five games from the affinity space's website, survey peers, and write reviews based on the survey data. |

Searching the internet can help you locate existing games. Visit game stores and speak with employees about ideal games; they often have suggestions and can help you contact affinity spaces. In addition, try the following. (Visit **go.SolutionTree.com/instruction** to access live links to the websites mentioned in this book.)

* Be a member of a network like Kongregate (www.kongregate.com), Games-Radar (www.gamesradar.com), GameStop Playlist (www.gamestop.com/collection/playlist), PC Gamer (www.pcgamer.com), or STEAM (http://store.steampowered.com).
* Visit free game sites like FOG (www.freeonlinegames.com), Friv (www.friv.com), Gamesgames.com (www.gamesgames.com), GirlsGoGames (www.girlsgogames.com), and Mousebreaker (www.mousebreaker.com) to see what is available. Evaluate these sites before students do to determine game appropriateness.

Some of the free games are created specifically for classroom use so teachers can target specific skills normally found in a K–12 curriculum. Their design is limited, as their purpose is to motivate student acquisition of a learning target by creating a highly structured experience with limited choices. These games are a good first step, but they are not enough by themselves to support a quest. Affinity spaces are crucial.

### Create to Learn

When designing games to learn, students embrace questions that they care about—questions about sustainability, social justice, happiness, natural resources, parenting, or economics, for example—and then craft experiences through gaming that lead other players to explore the same important questions. Game design success moves beyond meeting specific learning targets; it is interdisciplinary. Design includes mathematics for a rules system; psychology for a human play experience (such as how players will respond and interact when faced with a stimulus or decision, like in role-playing or character-driven games); social studies for cultural context; English language arts for storytelling, sequencing, and communicating; visual and audio performance for how objects, including characters, will move, make noises, and change, depending on game play; and technological literacy for computer programming.

A teacher might consider the following questions when a student proposes creating a game as a quest, and a quester might consider these questions when designing a game. Visit **go.SolutionTree.com/instruction** for a free reproducible version of these questions.

* What topics can I present through my game?
* What is the challenge or problem? What is the question?
* Why will players want to play this game?
* How many players will play at a time?
* How much time will it take to play this game?
* Where will they play the game?

* What do I want my players to learn while playing this game?
* What skills will my players use to reach a win state?
* How will players win this game?
* How will the world be a better place because players played this game?
* How will players feel while playing this game?
* Will players have fun?
* Why would someone want to play this game twice, three times, or one hundred times?
* How will I make sure players feel like they have choices and control?
* What will the players' identities be while they play this game, and are those identities positive?
* What existing games connect to this topic?
* Is this game appropriate for the learner?
* What will players learn from this game?
* What was the designer's purpose when he or she created this game?
* How long does it take to play this game?
* What skills does someone need to play this game?
* What equipment does someone need to play this game?
* What affinity spaces are dedicated to this interest or topic?
* How does the quester become a participant in these affinity spaces?

Because game design is such a complicated process, we suggest two resources that can provide a tutorial on design.

1. Games for Change (http://gamesforchange.org) features a competition and conference for games that promote positive themes and learning such as social justice, happiness, and world peace. The site has materials for every content area and every grade level. Each year, games with a positive impact earn awards. For example, Kognito showcases a game called *Start the Talk* at the conference to help parents and adults learn how to speak with teens about difficult topics. Its role play lets the player choose sentences, resulting in either a positive reaction from the simulated teen or a negative one in which the teen character leaves the conversation; other games include but aren't limited to *Blindside*, *Block'hood*, and *Reach for the Sun*. To design and submit a game to Games for Change for review might be a good quest for a student whose interests converge at social justice and programming.

2. *The Art of Game Design: A Book of Lenses, Second Edition* (Schell, 2015) provides a collection of over one hundred lenses—question sets—that help anyone trying to create a game consider all the facets that move the creator toward making a good game. From those lenses, we broke out these facets: purpose, impact, experience, rules, attraction, and form and structure.

Some categories' questions appear in the preceding list, but teacher-specific questions follow.

* Impact—What standards or content and skills do I want to teach a student? What is the desired impact—making our classroom a friendlier place, for instance?
* Experience—Will I exert high control or provide lots of latitude to the learner?
* Attraction—Will the game allow students to connect to one another in rare ways?

Games for Change and other apps and game sites like Schell Games, Code.org, Scratch (https://scratch.mit.edu), and GameSalad (http://gamesalad.com) offer modified, easy design tools ideal for beginners. Search for "game creator," "game-making software," "game studio," "game development," or "game make" online to find further websites that cater to everyone from novice game designer to expert.

Schell's (2015) work in virtual reality (also known as VR; www.schellgames.com/news/virtual-reality-in-the-classroom) and curriculum connections has taken questing to an exciting level. How is a student's quest to learn about atoms affected if he or she can actually see the environment using virtual reality? What happens if a student learning about graphing equations can feel the difference in the slope in a virtual reality roller-coaster experience?

Table 4.5 offers creation ideas for when students decide to design to learn.

**Table 4.5: Design Games to Learn**

| Content Area or Skill | Game Description |
|---|---|
| History | Students will design a game that teaches details about the French Revolution, including causes and major events. |
| Science, technology, engineering, mathematics | Students will design a game that teaches the player how to use physics to solve mazes. |
| Socio-emotional development | Students will design a game that simulates a conflict and teaches compromise so it can resolve as a win-win situation. |
| Mathematics | Students will design a game where the player must add and subtract fractions in a short time frame. |

How can you and your students find games and affinity spaces?

## Search for Affinity Spaces

Without affinity spaces, games are unlikely to connect to meaningful learning experiences. Affinity spaces are a tool with which you can build learning targets and network connections. It is possible to tap into affinity spaces that a gamer is familiar with or to suggest finding affinity spaces for games that are popular with a class. It is in the affinity spaces where learning goals come alive. For example, a class may play a board game in the classroom but then connect to an online forum discussion where players discuss tips, tricks, and strategies.

Because players typically play games outside an affinity space, the type of affinity space a player can access is wide open. It can be simple, perhaps at first including only interested class members instead of anyone outside the class. In this way, you can model and share protocols that explain how you want students to behave and communicate in an affinity space, and you are a gatekeeper for safety purposes. These ideas, combined with the tasks and feedback from the affinity space, can help with questing assessment, feedback, and reflection. In fact, in quests that choose elements of game design, assessments may be in the form of extended written responses or personal communications in affinity spaces.

With your students, think about where to find affinity spaces. Investigate links to forums or wikis that are on the game creator's website. Search online using the name of the game in the form of a question to find affinity spaces. Students who design a game can create an affinity space.

The disease questing example helps you imagine what a quest of game design looks like.

## Sample Questing Thread

This section continues the questing thread of disease as an example. Again, questing has learners identify their learning targets and their questions first. (Chapter 3, page 25, can help guide and form those questions.) Beyond that, teachers provide guidance based on student needs and strengths.

Decide if the learners will play a game to learn or design a game for other learners. A plethora of resources offer information and affinity spaces that align with the disease quest.

* **Consider learner as player:** Students could play *Pandemic* in the classroom, visit an affinity space dedicated to it (such as the forum on the BoardGameGeek [n.d.a; http://bit.ly/2rfTZEX]), and complete one of the following tasks.
    * Write an informational essay explaining how to quickly develop the cure when playing with four players, identifying each player's role.
    * Write an informational essay to post on the BoardGameGeek (n.d.c) forum for *Pandemic* (http://bit.ly/2tBa7l6) in response to a member asking how to win the game or as a discussion thread asking for feedback on the technique. If the information is high quality, the forum will often respond with a thank-you or other positive feedback. In the event of negative comments or distractions, students learn how to tactfully manage and deal with these things too. This feedback is from an authentic audience and can increase motivation and refine

learning targets as well as build independence and competence in communication skills.

* Compare classroom solutions and challenges with the forum discussion (BoardGameGeek, n.d.b; http://bit.ly/2ubb314). Participate in the discussions and craft answers to other members' problems if the class has a solution.

* Use accurate data tables that illustrate disease spread. In game play, include data tables as a critical element for reaching a win state.

* Document a strategy in play and evaluate its effectiveness. Include any changes for the next time players use it. Players can do this kind of process documentation individually or as a group.

* **Consider learner as game designer:** Students could design a game with two purposes.
   a. Help their game players understand how fast a disease can spread.
   b. Teach the players ways to avoid spreading diseases.

* **Consider learner as affinity space participant:** Students can engage with others to seek guidance. For example, the game *Pandemic* boasts the following affinity spaces.

   * Z-Man Games (www.zmangames.com/en/products/pandemic) offers adjustable difficulty and role exploration beyond the board game.

   * GamesDreams (n.d.; http://bit.ly/2tmQZak) is a resource that students can use to learn how to play and discuss strategy.

   * *Pandemic* YouTube (Z-Man Games, n.d.; http://bit.ly/2u6n2fi) is a channel that features video tutorials, strategy, and even challenges on video.

The following elementary, middle, and high school sections provide ideas to help shape quests and encourage teachers to envision possibilities for game design at different grade levels.

## Elementary School

Many of the elementary-level games focus on the basic biology of sickness. Themes like handwashing and courteous behaviors when we sneeze or prepare food dominate. Games that accompany hands-on activities like local museum or science center exhibits optimize learning.

Consider these games depending on the criteria we discussed earlier in this chapter regarding learning target, player age and readiness, skills, and interests. Table 4.6 (page 48) offers options for each game type.

**Table 4.6: Best-Fit Elementary Games for the Disease Quest**

| Content-Area Connections | Description | Game | Type |
|---|---|---|---|
| Biology | These games and resources will teach students about microbes and antibiotics. Students can visit e-Bug (www.e-bug.eu) to access additional games. | *Bogey Bus, Super Sneezes, Kitchen Mayhem, Stop the Spread, Chicken Surprise* | Cooperative |
| Microbiology (bacteria, viruses, parasites, epidemiology) | Students will learn about sickness, how it spreads, and how we can combat or prevent it. See Cambridge University's (n.d.) page Cambridge Infectious Diseases (http://bit.ly/2nsT9SB) for more microbiology games. | *Bug Battles* | Competitive |
| Biology (bacteria, viruses, parasites, epidemiology) | Students will investigate infectious disease mysteries by role playing various medical professionals. They can visit the *Disease Detectives* videos page (www.disease detectives.org/videos) to meet interactive patients, analyze lab tests, and learn about infectious disease transmission and prevention. | *Disease Detectives* | Simulation |

Elementary-level games stick mostly with basic concepts and graphics.

## Middle School

Middle school games present a higher level of complexity and present issues and content associated with diseases. Students begin to look at global impacts and the process involved in preventing a pandemic as a society.

Consider these games depending on the criteria we discussed earlier in this chapter regarding learning target, player age and readiness, skills, and interests. Table 4.7 offers options for each game type.

## High School

Games at the high school level present issues and content attached to the science of pathogens and pandemics. They look deeper at the biology, chemistry, and sociology behind the spread and attempts to prevent spreading diseases. The challenge at the high school level is to maintain fun and engagement with the richer content. Table 4.8 offers options for each game type.

**Table 4.7: Best-Fit Middle School Games for the Disease Quest**

| Content-Area Connections | Description | Game | Type |
|---|---|---|---|
| Problem solving, collaboration, history, biology, geography, vocabulary | Between two and four students will choose roles and work together to cure diseases that threaten world regions. Students can visit the GamesDreams (n.d.) site (http://bit .ly/2tmQZak) to play online. | *Pandemic* | Cooperative |
| Logic, attention to textual details, vocabulary, problem solving, decision making | Students will use their problem-solving skills to resolve an outbreak with this CDC-created game. Students can access the game on the CDC's (n.d.a) site (http://bit .ly/292UDhu) to play. | *Solve the Outbreak* | Competitive |
| Biology (bacteria, viruses, parasites, epidemiology) | Students will investigate infectious disease mysteries by role playing various medical professionals. Participants access *Disease Detectives* videos (www.diseasedetectives.org/videos) to meet interactive patients, analyze lab tests, and learn how to transmit and prevent infectious diseases. | *Disease Detectives* | Simulation |

**Table 4.8: Best-Fit High School Games for the Disease Quest**

| Content-Area Connections | Description | Game | Type |
|---|---|---|---|
| Biology, chemistry, genetics | Students will learn about and compare genomes from various species in this interactive game. (*Solve the Outbreak* is also a helpful game to connect biology and chemistry to gaming.) | *Phylo the DNA Puzzle Game* | Cooperative |
| Sciences including microbiology, technology, engineering, mathematics | These games from Cambridge University are appropriate for middle and high school students. Students will investigate the causes and effects of various diseases. | *The Great Flu Game, Power of Research, Gut Infection, Medical Mysteries, Killer Flu, Pandemic II* | Competitive |

continued ➡

| Content-Area Connections | Description | Game | Type |
|---|---|---|---|
| Life sciences | This series of games offers open-access mazes for students of all ages, but especially older learners, to tap their knowledge of fundamental science concepts so they can exit a maze. | *MazeFire Digital Maze Games* | Competitive |
| Biology, chemistry | Students will investigate an epidemiologic case study. | *Pharyngitis in Louisiana* | Simulation |

High school–level games offer deep study in content areas. See ScienceGameCenter (n.d.; http://bit.ly/2t9WHJ6) for other games dealing with disease. (Visit **go.Solution Tree.com/instruction** to access live links to the websites mentioned in this book.)

## Coda

This chapter explained how a good game design takes the challenge of a worthy problem and creates a learning experience around it. By setting learning targets via inquiry, students can design or play different game types, including cooperative, competitive, and simulation, or any combination of all three. Our hope is that you will consider the options we presented here and set a goal for using game design, combined with an affinity space, to achieve meaningful learning.

# CHAPTER 5

# Building Connections With Network Design

Lying at the heart of network design are the tenets of engagement that involve participating in an active, intentional cycle with clear goals and right-sized, actionable steps while participating in social, collaborative opportunities that grow expertise.

Through network design, students investigate and analyze problems within a cadre of physical and virtual interactors (students, teachers, and social media participants, including invited experts). Students can connect to a network, communicate and collaborate with a local or global team, know when to plug into different networks and network participants, and utilize their networks for feedback and reflection to access multiple perspectives and resources.

To effectively nurture this focus, teachers and students must intentionally make network design choices that invite higher-order thinking and collaboration. Finding others with whom to share something that is emotionally gripping can foster commitment. Researchers find that collaboration's value "may be due in large part to the metacognitive benefit of having peers examine and comment upon one's thinking" (Partnership for 21st Century Learning, 2016, p. 4). Social media, from Facebook and Twitter to Instagram and Snapchat, creates places where people can virtually connect to others who share common interests. When you invite networks into your classroom, students soon realize that sharing via their networks is an aspect of the overall quest.

This chapter focuses on network space types—physical, plus, public, member, and mentor—and how students can decide which is the best one for them to engage with when they are designing their quests. The design's complexity may require a teacher to make explicit curriculum and school goal connections to the network design approach. This is not a step-by-step plan with strict parameters; it's a fluid zone in which the student, as the driver, navigates the necessary network depending on task, purpose, and audience. This chapter also addresses foundational network concerns and continues the sample disease questing thread via network design.

## Curriculum and School Goals

Before exploring the five network spaces, we want to clarify *why* network design is worth the complexity. The abilities to work together to raise questions, take action, and examine results are key to student learning. Students develop rich understandings of the content as well as hone skills vital to the subject area. For example, the National Council for the Social Studies' (2013) *College, Career and Civic Life (C3) Framework for Social Studies State Standards* promotes:

> Active and responsible citizens [who] identify and analyze public problems; deliberate with other people about how to define and address issues; take constructive, collaborative action; reflect on their actions; create and sustain groups; and influence institutions both large and small . . . Individual mastery of content often no longer suffices; students should also develop the capacity to work together to apply knowledge to real problems. (p. 19)

The Next Generation Science Standards (NGSS Lead States, 2013) articulate a learning model that values the practices of scientists and engineers as they engage in their disciplines. The Common Core English language arts standards advocate for students to have:

> Ample opportunities to take part in a variety of rich, structured conversations [and this] requires that students contribute accurate, relevant information; respond to and develop what others have said; make comparisons and contrasts; and analyze and synthesize a multitude of ideas in various domains. (NGA & CCSSO, 2010b)

Collectively pursuing the ability to articulate compelling questions and the iterative design of an investigation, a prototype, or an idea creates a community of learners within and beyond the classroom. Desirable employability skills such as adaptability and collaboration are in the forefront as students connect with members in pursuit of relevant, worthy inquiries and interesting or emotionally gripping experiences (Breene, 2016; Wagner, 2008). Students interact in formal learning spaces that a teacher or physical or virtual members working on a project organize, as well as in informal learning spaces that students find or create to achieve an objective.

This type of learning and the spaces in which the learning occurs are predicated on disrupting tradition (or at least disrupting traditional classroom actions). Many teachers are already using *I can* statements to clarify standards-based learning targets in student-friendly language. We also propose the delineation of *We can* statements like those that follow to indicate standards-based and dispositional member goals.

* "We can investigate the niches of different butterflies and compare their roles in their habitats."

&ast; "We can learn more about the global refugee crisis and collaborate with global organizations to provide refugee assistance."

Now we delineate the kinds of spaces where students network.

## Network Space Types

Network spaces are part of the second engagement tenet's right-sized zone. *Right sized* in this case means students access these spaces when they need them, including when they are ready to move their growing expertise up a level. As students get older and become increasingly skilled at using digital tools, they have more opportunities for engaging with others beyond the classroom. They may engage with others in different ways based on need, interest, or objective. These spaces can vary for ideal access and to meet the student's just-in-time needs.

Table 5.1 introduces the different spaces and offers an at-a-glance reference.

**Table 5.1: Network Design Spaces**

| Network Space | Definition | Example |
|---|---|---|
| Physical | A physical space is a networking space that the teacher designs and manages for student use. | Examples include classrooms, media centers, and computer labs; physical spaces are less likely to include internet tools in favor of existing software on local computers. |
| Plus | This space, which expands a physical space, invites virtual networking. The teacher drives the decisions for inviting additional virtual resources. | These spaces include Skype, Twitter hashtag searches, and protected social spaces like Edmodo and Schoology. |
| Public | This physical and virtual networking space offers access to physical and virtual resources as well as flexible furniture in a place that allows reconfiguration, which can change depending on the task. Students manipulate physical and plus spaces; they drive the discovery of additional needed resources and information and have the autonomy to do so. | Expanded online resources, including social media, are common in public spaces. These spaces can occur outside of school and may extend to libraries, community centers, or other places that fit a task, which students determine. Learners might decide to attend a cultural fair in another city or participate in an online conference broadcast from another country. |

continued ➧

| Network Space | Definition | Example |
|---|---|---|
| Member | This is the first level of an affinity space. There is purposeful flow and feedback occurring between physical and virtual spaces via networks like LISTSERVs, social media, content-specific chat rooms, and content-specific websites that allow communication (perhaps through comments). Learners actively seek out existing networks and resources across all spaces and access those resources depending on their just-in-time needs. | Students could create an online group on Facebook or Schoology to collaborate in both inside and outside of school. They may leave comments or questions on a YouTube channel, a wiki, or a Reddit thread as they seek information and resources. |
| Mentor | This is the second level of an affinity space. A mentor space specifically seeks out those with demonstrated and vetted credentials, and those who create multifaceted curated (expert vetted and collected) resources or moderate (lead in the spaces that students might seek out) member spaces. | Experts here could include other teachers, scientists, and historians—any expert in a particular field. These mentors could be available physically or virtually depending on geographic location or availability. These experts might be students; an expert is anyone who demonstrates credentials. The expert, in general, just needs to play the role of someone who knows more than the learner and help the learner improve or refine his or her learning. |

The following sections detail each type of space, including physical, plus, public, member, and mentor, the last two of which are affinity spaces.

## Physical Space

This is not necessarily the four-walls-and-five-rows-of-desks classroom. A *physical space* is a learning space that teachers and students can design to serve diverse tasks and support more student-centered or open-ended learning experiences. When schools start thinking of upgrading the physical space, they may want to consider flexible furniture options and spaces that invite collaboration and comfort. The physical space may change. The physical space might include students in a remote location like a field trip, or it could mean moving to another area of a school like a laboratory or auditorium. The physical space lives within plus, member, and mentor spaces because students also need to access areas and devices where they can plug into virtual opportunities.

## Plus Space

The *plus space* extends the physical space to invite virtual networking. This invitation could extend to a teacher in another country, an expert in the quest topic, or access to any online resource currently available. As teacher, you largely control the plus space, but you might solicit student input on additional resources to increase their choices and buy-in.

Note that in the plus space, educators still use physical spaces to house the exploration into a given topic, challenge, or problem. As students begin to take the lead on virtual opportunities, they start moving into public, member, and mentor spaces.

## Public Space

The *public space* is an intentional and dynamic physical or virtual space that students and teachers can redesign and rearrange depending on the task. Furniture and technology vary, and everyone has access to this space. This space includes the physical and plus spaces, but it is not teacher controlled. In public spaces, the teacher begins relinquishing control to the students as they make their own intentional and right-sized decisions, though the teacher may still guide and coach students through choices and access to additional resources.

The public space has many types of virtual networking opportunities, including access to essential, relevant resources as well as other students, teachers, experts, and anyone who can offer guidance toward a solution or provide information. Students and teachers share the decision making about opportunities for virtual networking.

Schools are starting to shift their notions about spaces by integrating the physical and the virtual. Libraries, computer labs, and production rooms are being absorbed either by the traditional classroom space or in modern spaces designed to provide access to all media and resources with flexible furniture and multiple ways to reshape the spaces. A public space is a lot like a coffee shop that has flexible seating arrangements and free Wi-Fi. It can function as just a coffee shop, or it can easily transform into a meeting space for whoever needs it. It can be the place where experts or interest groups converge in person or virtually, and it serves everyone's needs.

## Member Space

*Member spaces* are the first level of affinity spaces (Gee & Hayes, 2011). James Paul Gee and Elisabeth Hayes (2011) say that "while people may eventually come to value their fellow members as one of the primary reasons for being in the affinity space, the shared passion is foregrounded as the reason for being there" (p. 9).

Physical and virtual member spaces are dynamic and intentional, authentically representing the task's demands and the needs of all involved. Unlike physical member spaces, however, virtual member spaces are intuitive rather than planned and are student directed. These spaces are responsive to just-in-time student needs, and the student initiates the need. Member spaces include physical, plus, and public spaces. They are differentiated from public spaces because the student, at this level, independently knows where to seek out needed information.

Member spaces are where a strong toolbox or repertoire of resources is vitally important. This is where being strategic and capable matters. Students in a member space use all available resources, including a vast array of digital tools, traditional physical texts, and physical and human interactions for mainly student-directed tasks. Students may be researching, investigating, and learning collaboratively but have the autonomy to diverge, explore, and develop peripheral skills related to their quests.

As an example of member spaces, students who play *Minecraft* quickly learn that the basic game has limits. They can overcome those limitations if they learn how to create game modifications. The student must seek out those with knowledge about modification creation. Sometimes they do this through social media, but in our experience, they often search YouTube, Reddit (if the student is in high school), or a forum associated with *Minecraft* modifications. Whoever creates the YouTube video, posts in the forum, or does an AMA (ask me anything) on Reddit becomes, for the moment, a member of that student's affinity space.

## Mentor Space

The *mentor space*, the second level of affinity spaces, is where learners solicit information and feedback from the space's expert or professional members or from someone with vetted credentials. For instance, students working on a project about space travel would normally start (and probably end) with resources in their school's physical library. But questing students might reach out via social media or email to a scientist at NASA. The students have now reached out to and brought in an expert to join their affinity space. The expert remains during the students' needs and then leaves the affinity space.

This is also a space where the learned individuals may be students—particularly those who have been valued community members in a learning or member space for a long period of time, and who have built trust and demonstrated essential expertise to other members. Students often create tutorials and forums. Some have built a following of many members, depending on the quality of their online contributions and the trustworthiness they've established within their own networks.

## Network Concerns

These open spaces do have some caveats that require addressing. Communicating and collaborating with a global network of peers, experts, and resources comes with legitimate concerns about online safety, ethical content use, and validity of sources and network collaborators. To revise the popular Spider-Man quote, with great global access comes great global responsibility.

For many students, interacting with each other physically and virtually is second nature, but these students don't always make the best decisions for themselves or their academic tasks. They still need modeling, guidance, and support from you so they can make appropriate choices. Safety, ethical content use, and source validity are foundational networking aspects to consider during this type of quest design. The contemporary skills of media literacy and accountability (Jacobs & Alcock, 2017; Partnership for 21st Century Learning, n.d.) relate to and rely on all these aspects.

### Safety

Online safety is paramount in education, particularly when students are engaging new network participants, experts, and others around the globe. What should teachers do to keep students safe online? How do teachers honor that safety without stifling or limiting learning? They should:

* Teach students to question and report dubious behavior and content
* Monitor their interactions and give support and guidance when something looks wrong
* Model potential unsafe scenarios and how students should handle them
* Praise and reward students' good decision-making skills
* Communicate transparently with parents about what their children will access, and how unsafe scenarios can be powerful teaching moments rather than opportunities for scolding and punishment

Common Sense Media (www.commonsensemedia.org) has more information on internet safety. (Visit **go.SolutionTree.com/instruction** to access live links to the websites mentioned in this book.)

### Ethical Content Use

Inviting students into new spaces and collaborations with global partners means that guidance on ethical content use is essential. Plagiarism is one ethics issue. Students must learn to avoid intentionally or unintentionally using images, movie clips, or sound bites without giving credit to the creator. Students need to know that any sort of copying without attribution is wrong.

To keep students in the right ethical headspaces, consider the following teacher actions.

* **Demand attribution for every piece of media, no matter how small:** Teach students that their work is incomplete without citations. Teach students that just because something appears online doesn't mean that it's free for them to use. If they didn't create it, they must cite it or ask permission to use it.
* **Teach students the different types of work to give credit to an original author or artist for:** Cite direct quotes, paraphrased material, images, and digital presentations and movies. The author or artist's information may appear on the image, in a list of credits at the end of a digital work, or on a

cover or title page of a printed work. There are myriad ways to give credit, including following Modern Language Association or American Psychological Association style.

* **Show students how to read and use a Creative Commons license:** Students can use these licenses (https://creativecommons.org/licenses) to receive free distribution permissions to use content (though attribution is still mandatory), without infringing on copyright. There are different versions of these licenses, and students would benefit from knowing them all.

* **Explain how users may purchase some media:** Images and sound bites are usually available to purchase for a nominal fee. Students can use them in their work.

* **Inform students that material posted online is visible to everyone:** If they are sharing work online, it is an act of public publishing. Their work is more visible to a wider audience, meaning they are liable for their citations and attributions.

The Global Digital Citizen Foundation (n.d.; https://globaldigitalcitizen.org) has more information on *digital citizenship*, that is "engaging in appropriate and exemplary behaviour in an online environment." Authors Lee Watanabe Crockett and Andrew Churches (2017) go even further in their book *Growing Global Digital Citizens* and define *global digital citizenship* as "how we participate and contribute in the blended physical and digital worlds, and how we can leverage the digital world to grow citizens in this new reality" (p. 4).

## Source Validity

How does a student know what to believe, and how does he or she verify the truth? Students in particular are likely to be more susceptible to unsupported internet claims. In a Stanford University study, professor of education and history Sam Wineburg finds that 80–90 percent of the 7,800 students it asked to evaluate online articles and news sources struggled to judge the credibility of the news they read (as cited in McEvers, 2016). Some sources are intentionally misleading and exist only to propagate misinformation. The prevalence of online misinformation spawned the website Snopes (www.snopes.com), which provides evidence to support or dismiss claims. Similar sites, such as PolitiFact (www.politifact.com), have appeared since to address claims that politicians make and look for evidence to support those claims.

Teachers can consider the following, culled from working with teachers and students, to help students verify and validate information.

* **Intuition:** Student has a feeling or sense about the resources or experts he or she is in contact with.
  * Does the resource seem off or misleading?
  * Is the resource wildly different from other resources?
  * Did some special interest pay for the inclusion of a resource? (That alone doesn't invalidate a resource, but does raise a red flag.)

* **Authoritative connection:** Student looks for related affiliation information about the resources or experts.
  * Is there an apparent author? What else has the author created?
  * What is the author's background, and how does that relate to his or her reliability or objectivity?
  * Is the domain a mostly trustworthy one, such as .org, .edu, or .gov, or is it associated with a more questionable domain such as .com, .biz, or .coop?
* **Verifiable details:** Student compares details from a resource to alternative sources and primary documents to verify its details.
  * Does the resource include references or links?
  * Are claims supported with citations to other related resources?
  * Are there authoritative connections, such as direct, sourced quotes?

As students learn to navigate these network spaces, they are learning key critical- and creative-thinking skills, collecting data and drawing conclusions, and solving problems.

## Sample Questing Thread

The following sections offer network space ideas in relation to the quest topic example of disease. Since diseases can be both private and public conversations, students must consider how far their networks need to extend to ensure the highest levels of learning. Students new to questing may need more guidance when initially navigating resources and limitations to physical, plus, or public spaces, and when it's time to extend the work into more sophisticated member and mentor spaces. Teachers decide on network spaces based on students' ages and readiness, as well as available resources. To that end, apply the following questions to determine potential network spaces. Visit **go.SolutionTree .com/instruction** for a free reproducible version of these questions.

* Who has the information we need?
* Can we gather information in our classroom? How else can we gather information—through phone calls, on social media, or online?
* Can we use the internet for action purposes?
* How do we network for information without causing a panic?
* Who knows more about this?
* How do we manage misinformation?
* How do we verify sources?
* Who needs our information?
* What networks should we start reaching out to?

The examples are not necessarily associated with elementary, middle, or high school singularly, and they vary depending on location and a school's available resources. The following sections offer resource ideas by network space type.

### Physical Space Ideas

The teacher likely directs the research opportunities and provides materials, which include resources that already exist in the classroom, a school's media center, or a computer lab.

* Books about diseases
* Print and online encyclopedias for disease-related articles
* Software, databases, and school-based network programs, like Learn360 (https://learn360.infobase.com) or BioMedia Project (http://biomediaproject .com/bmp); and other library media hubs such as Reading Rainbow (www. readingrainbow.com), Quality Assurance International (www.qai-inc.com), Meridian Health Services (www.meridianhs.org), Global Wonders (www. globalwonders.com), University of Cambridge (www.cam.ac.uk), and MARSHmedia (https://marshmedia.com), which give access to disease-related media

### Plus Space Ideas

Research opportunities are still likely teacher directed, but there is flexibility to connect online in new ways. For instance, you might reach out on Twitter or Facebook to ask a question related to student research or reach out to another teacher, an author, or a scientist. As students get into middle school, teachers may want to consider relinquishing some control to students for expanding the physical spaces, where they self-select new plus spaces based on their quests independent of the teacher.

* Protected social spaces using tools like Edmodo (www.edmodo.com) and Schoology (www.schoology.com) for collection and curation of online disease resources
* Skype (www.skype.com) or Around the World With 80 Schools (http:// aroundtheworldwith80schools.net) to find teachers all over the globe who are teaching about diseases
* Google Hangouts (https://hangouts.google.com) or Skype conversations with experts, other teachers and students, or anyone else who can offer information on disease in general or specific diseases
* Distance learning setups or virtual field trips with colleges or professors who specialize in diseases, government agencies that respond to disease threats, or museums associated with disease or human pathology, such as the University of Sydney's Pathology Museum or Koshland Science Museum's Infectious Disease exhibit
* Twitter hashtag searches and conversations, from the general #diseases to the specific #cancer, #zika, or #aids

## Public Space Ideas

Both student- and teacher-directed research opportunities use a variety of planned and unplanned social and connective tools. Additionally, students decide how they will use their learning spaces in terms of layout and functionality.

* Students have access to many types of social media and actively engage it to learn about diseases, question their networks for disease-related information and media, analyze network-suggested resources, vet information, focus their work, and curate their search results.
* Students make decisions around hashtag searches, including seeking out those entities (people and organizations) that actively work with diseases, and perhaps following those entities and creating user groups that discuss and share information about diseases on various types of social media.
* Students may continue using in-school resources as well as local resources such as government entities, libraries, businesses, historical places, science labs, and museums.

## Member Space Ideas

In member spaces, students make decisions about whom to contact and how to connect with the right people. Students share items such as survey results, new learning about diseases and access to diagnostic information, and information related to cures.

* Students contact representatives from a distinguished organization such as the CDC, the World Health Organization (WHO; www.who.int/en), or a pharmacological manufacturing company. Students run ideas, scenarios, and prototypes through the experts in this member space to solicit feedback such as whether their pathogenic projections are on target or whether their disaster readiness plan needs additional information.
* Students consult existing media, such as YouTube videos—particularly from someone or a group that generates multiple videos—or a wiki that was collaboratively created around diseases in general or around a specific disease.
* Students check existing disease-focused networks, such as the Undiagnosed Diseases Network (https://undiagnosed.hms.harvard.edu) or the National Organization for Rare Disorders (https://rarediseases.org). Individuals within these networks might move the learning into a mentor space.

## Mentor Space Ideas

Student-directed and highly collaborative mentor spaces are where students seek expertise and their own coaching opportunities. They may become coaches themselves as they interact with others and share the information they have learned about diseases.

Students can engage in multifaceted network opportunities that include engaging in several networks at once or deeply engaging in a particular network, particularly if the research has a focal point around a specific disease or a specific angle like curing or managing the outbreak. This may lead students to seek out the following resources.

* Students contact specific scientists, lab personnel, doctors, or researchers. Students run ideas, scenarios, and prototypes through the experts in this member space to solicit feedback such as whether their pathogenic projections are on target or whether their disaster readiness plan needs additional information.

* Students invite organizations such as the CDC, the American Cancer Society (www.cancer.org), and WHO to join their affinity spaces.

The following elementary, middle, and high school sections give ideas to help shape quests and encourage teachers to envision possibilities for network design at different grade levels.

## Elementary School

When students are in elementary school, they must learn foundational skills before adeptly moving into more sophisticated spaces. Many online spaces have minimum-age limits for this reason.

It is perfectly logical for elementary students and teachers to hang out in primarily physical and plus spaces, or for teachers to actively engage additional spaces with a classroom-level social media account or group-decided hashtag. You can vet and gather online information resources in a LiveBinders (www.livebinders.com) binder, which allows users to organize online video links or other resources. Students can visit Symbaloo (www.symbaloo.com) to research multiple vetted sources that the teacher has bookmarked.

## Middle School

Middle school students can quickly move well beyond the physical and plus spaces that elementary students can access. It's acceptable to root network space explorations in the physical and plus spaces first, letting students develop foundational knowledge before they plug into additional spaces. Students may have ideas and questions that the teacher didn't plan for but are still worth exploring through public, member, and mentor spaces.

When moving into public spaces such as reimagined classrooms or redesigned instructional spaces with multiple-resource accessibility, flexible furniture, and multiple types of Wi-Fi-connected devices, where teachers *and* students co-direct the interactions, students begin to get their first taste of intellectual freedom. The more interactions students have and the more spaces students work in, the higher quality their work will be.

### High School

High school network space interactions are likely to be similar to those in middle school but may offer deeper opportunities for work in the member and mentor spaces. As an example, the National Institutes of Health's ongoing research program supplies grants that educational entities can apply for. These grants provide funds to create partnerships between schools and colleges for programs that enhance diversity in the biomedical, behavioral, and clinical research workforce. In this case, students join a cohort that may or may not be students from their home schools. They work with this cohort during the program for both in-person gatherings and virtual interactions with their team—member spaces. Each student, or pair of students, pairs with a working scientist who becomes his or her mentor. This person is physically with the students in lab scenarios, helping with research and procedures. They connect virtually through diverse technologies, including email, blogs, social media, and webinars—mentor spaces.

Johni Cruse-Craig, of the national Delta Teacher Efficacy Campaign, and Hadiyah-Nicole Green, assistant professor of physiology at the Morehouse School of Medicine, share how important it is for contemporary students to feel supported both in and out of the classroom, through a variety of ways to connect. "Real science happens through modeling, describing, and explaining with both peers and teachers or mentors and constant support offers continued engagement and opportunities for discovery," Green asserts (personal communication, February 22, 2017). Cruse-Craig adds, "In our learning landscape, with all the ways in which we can connect, we have an obligation to ensure that our instructional programs match the types of interactions that students are having in the real world" (personal communication, February 22, 2017).

## Coda

This chapter made the case for why network design choices are fundamental to seeking out and sharing information and ideas. Engaging in multiple network spaces affords all students opportunities to break free of traditional education constructs. By learning about the network spaces we discuss in this chapter (physical, plus, public, member, and mentor), teachers can help students broaden access to expertise and enhance collaborative opportunities. Engaging students in networking choices keeps them engaged, and it supports short- and long-term learning goals. This chapter also discussed network concerns of safety, ethical use, and validity. If we want students to connect to these different spaces, we have to ensure that we are doing so in ways that are authentic, meaningful, innovative, creative, and safe. Contemporary students are likely already connecting to a multitude of people and resources. It's time to use those social connections to our advantage for deeper learning.

PART II
# Guiding

# CHAPTER 6

# Launching the Quest

This chapter leverages your existing realities as an educator to reimagine a learning journey, focusing on topics that are worthy of questing. Author and curriculum expert Heidi Hayes Jacobs equates curriculum design to a "creative writing endeavor" that requires inquiring and posing problems, innovating and imagining, and thinking flexibly (personal communication, May 3, 2016).

Look at your current curriculum, assessments, and instructional designs. Do they teach students how to lead? Do they teach students how to solve interesting problems (Godin, 2010)? These questions help develop a new culture of classroom connections. Consider the following questions as well.

* What decisions are students currently making? Are students acting as receivers or explorers?
* Are students interested in the problems they are solving and projects they are doing?
* What degree of authenticity does my classroom have? What about authenticity of student work?
* What promotes student decision making during exploration and evaluation?

Here we examine familiar resources for curriculum inspiration: standards, curriculum-unit maps, textbooks, mission statements, current events, and your students. We then leverage familiar design structures to articulate learning goals and ideas that help students demonstrate learning. Many students will need help charting their quests' paths. Teachers can guide them by providing curriculum inspiration for quest topics, challenge clarification, standards mapping, and deliverable determination, as this chapter explains. The disease example questing thread provides several curriculum-unit templates, which help students and teachers articulate the challenge and goals.

## Design Decisions to Guide the Quest

Teachers guide students through the series of design decisions that figure 6.1 delineates. Teachers invite students to consider the following questions when first charting the course.

| Decision One: Topic or Challenge Criteria (Chapters 6 and 7) | |
|---|---|
| Focus:<br>✦ Problem, purpose, challenge, or meaningful idea<br>✦ Non-negotiable learning targets<br>✦ Possible goals and topics of interest | Probing questions to ask students:<br>✦ "Why does this matter?"<br>✦ "What would you like to be able to do six weeks from now that you cannot do today?"<br>✦ "What does this mean to you?"<br>✦ "Have you thought about the impact you will have creating this?"<br>✦ "What other thoughts do you have about it?"<br>✦ "What is the opportunity here?"<br>✦ "What is the challenge?" |
| **Decision Two: Question Design (Chapter 3)** | |
| Focus:<br>✦ Essential question<br>✦ Driving questions | Probing questions to ask with students:<br>✦ "What issues or problems do you see here?"<br>✦ "How long have you been thinking about this?"<br>✦ "How can you find out?"<br>✦ "What do you want to ask?"<br>✦ "What other questions do you have about it?"<br>✦ "What is here that you want to explore?"<br>✦ "What is your approach to developing the idea?" |
| **Decision Three: Game Design (Chapter 4)** | |
| Focus:<br>✦ Play or create<br>✦ Game type<br>✦ Existing games<br>✦ Affinity spaces | Probing questions to ask with students:<br>✦ "Tell me what possibilities for action you see. Do not worry yet if they are realistic."<br>✦ "What possibilities have you seen used?"<br>✦ "What is the experience you are looking to create?"<br>✦ "What story do you want to tell?"<br>✦ "How would you teach this part?"<br>✦ "How can you make this more fun?"<br>✦ "How do you want it to be?" |
| **Decision Four: Network Design (Chapter 5)** | |
| Focus:<br>✦ Physical spaces<br>✦ Plus spaces<br>✦ Public spaces<br>✦ Member spaces<br>✦ Mentor spaces | Probing questions to ask with students:<br>✦ "Who might be able to help?"<br>✦ "Whom did you help?"<br>✦ "Who is able to help you?"<br>✦ "Who else will benefit?"<br>✦ "Who else would care about this?"<br>✦ "What is the effect on others?"<br>✦ "What resources are available to you?" |

| Decision Five: Timeline and Action Plan (Chapter 8) | |
|---|---|
| Focus:<br>✧ Practicing items<br>✧ Assessing networks<br>✧ Identifying and monitoring deliverable's due date | Probing questions to ask with students:<br>✧ "How much time do you need to do this?"<br>✧ "How does this fit with your plans?"<br>✧ "What do you need to succeed here?"<br>✧ "Do you have a detailed strategy to get there?"<br>✧ "What is the action plan?"<br>✧ "Who is your target audience?"<br>✧ "What are you really looking forward to doing?"<br>✧ "What is holding you back?"<br>✧ "Is this goal pulling you forward, or are you struggling to reach it?"<br>✧ "What is the first step you need to take to reach your goal?" |
| Decision Six: Commitment Statement (Chapter 8) | |
| Focus:<br>✧ Commitment language<br>✧ Commitment roles (*I* language and *We* language) | Probing questions to ask with students:<br>✧ "How do you feel about learning this?"<br>✧ "Is anything holding you back?"<br>✧ "What are you willing to do to make this happen?"<br>✧ "What do you think will be easy for you?"<br>✧ "What do you think will be challenging for you?"<br>✧ "What are you responsible for here?" |
| Decision Seven: Checkpoints (Chapter 8) | |
| Focus:<br>✧ Purpose<br>✧ Timeline for feedback checkpoints | Probing questions to ask with students:<br>✧ "What has occurred since we last spoke?"<br>✧ "What would you like to talk about?"<br>✧ "What did you accomplish?"<br>✧ "To what extent are you on track to meet your goals?"<br>✧ "What is happening now (what, where, when, who, how much, how often, and what do you see)?" |
| Decision Eight: Formative Assessment Design (Chapter 8) | |
| Focus:<br>✧ Targets<br>✧ Assessment methods for determining feedback<br>✧ Activities, learning strategies, and checkpoint items | Probing questions to ask with students:<br>✧ "What do you feel you can do right now? Can you practice or learn something new?"<br>✧ "How much energy to learn do you have right now?"<br>✧ "What do you need to practice?"<br>✧ "What do you still need to learn?"<br>✧ "What small steps can you take to get you closer to your goal?"<br>✧ "Which step can you take that will make the biggest difference right now?"<br>✧ "If we could wipe the slate clean, what would you do?" |
| Decision Nine: Feedback (Chapter 8) | |

Figure 6.1: Quest decisions.

continued ➡

| Focus: | Probing questions to ask with students: |
|---|---|
| ✧ Feedback timeline<br>✧ Feedback format<br>✧ Feedback audience or source | ✧ "What is your desired outcome?"<br>✧ "If you get it, what will you have?"<br>✧ "How will you know you have reached it?"<br>✧ "What will it look like? How did you determine this to be true?"<br>✧ "If I were in your shoes and asked for advice, what is the first thing you would tell me?"<br>✧ "Is this what you want to work on?"<br>✧ "Is this giving you energy, joy, or happiness or taking it away?"<br>✧ "What is holding you back?"<br>✧ "On a scale of one to ten, ten being proudest, how proud of your work are you right now?"<br>✧ "When do I need this feedback to keep going forward?" |
| **Decision Ten: Deliverables (Chapter 9)** | |
| Focus:<br>✧ Deliverable form<br>✧ Deliverable criteria | Probing questions to ask with students:<br>✧ "Is this the best outcome you can imagine, or is there something greater?"<br>✧ "What did you learn?"<br>✧ "What really stood out to you through this process? Can you share that with others somehow?"<br>✧ "What does quality look like?" |
| **Decision Eleven: Closure (Chapter 9)** | |
| Focus:<br>✧ Elements for celebration<br>✧ Elements for next steps<br>✧ Expert confirmation | Probing questions to ask with students:<br>✧ "What was your biggest win of this process?"<br>✧ "How will you celebrate that?"<br>✧ "What are you grateful for?"<br>✧ "Who is grateful for you?"<br>✧ "If you could do it over again, what would you do differently?"<br>✧ "What is next for you?" |

# Inspiration Sourcing

There are many sources for inspiration—students, standards, curriculum-unit maps, textbooks, school mission statements or themes, and current events. Each source is described with that versatility in mind.

## Students

It's always ideal for teachers to know who their students are—where they are from, what they imagine, what they care about, and what their worries are. Background knowledge and personal aspirations are good quests because they are relevant for students.

You could try the approach that Brian Durst (https://formofthegood.wordpress.com), a high school English teacher in Wisconsin, regularly takes. Durst (2015) asks the following three questions to help students co-create.

1. "What if?" (See the power of possibility.)
2. "Why not?" (Grant yourself permission.)
3. "So what?" (Create something original, significant, or enduring.)

If you apply these questions to something that interests students, the results might look like the following.

* Teachers help students build background knowledge about the ocean and its distinct layers, from the pelagic to the abyssal and hadal zones.
* During the initial instruction to build background and conceptual knowledge, a student offers a news tidbit related to salt lakes underneath the ocean. The student wonders what that means. The teacher and student both wonder, "*What if* we diverge from the current background-building path and instead focus on learning about lakes underneath the ocean?"
* The students wonder, "Why not?" as the topic piques their interest about something that they've never heard before, lives outside their understanding, and is beyond the current foundational focus.
* The students end up investigating recent news articles about briny lakes beneath the ocean on the floor of the Gulf of Mexico. They begin to research the occurrence of brine lakes and rivers in the abyssal and hadal zones.
* Students find that *So what?* revolves around the acquired peripheral information that they would not have otherwise learned in the previous learning sequence. Also, it offers opportunities for ways they will ultimately share and demonstrate their learning. Will they pursue research that contributes to the current information bank? Will they seek out those with expertise to guide them? Will they become experts who provide information to others who are learning about the same topic? Will they continue asking questions and learning?

Engage them in assignments where they reveal fictional and real-life heroes, challenges they have overcome, or their concerns. Have students take the lead recording information in a journal, but clarify that you will peruse what they write to help make learning meaningful and worthwhile.

## Standards

Standards introductions often have rich content to inspire quests. Starting a quest at the standard level begins with questions about how the teacher and the students interpret the standard. On coming to a common understanding, the questions can shift to what students are working toward.

For example, to introduce educators, parents, and community members to the Next Generation Science Standards, NGSS Lead States (2013) make the case that much of public policy and daily life require a certain level of engineering and scientific knowledge, such as "selecting among alternative medical treatments or determining how to invest public funds for water supply options." You can launch a quest by examining a given disease or condition and including promising medical practices from both Eastern and Western medicine (to address the alternative medical treatments). Another quest can focus on technologies and maximizing urban areas' savings by capturing stormwater or distilling seawater.

Likewise, the Common Core English language arts standards clarify significant shifts by delineating what students should be able to do according to the standards. In reading, for example, students should be prepared to:

> Readily undertake the close, attentive reading that is at the heart of understanding and enjoying complex works of literature; habitually perform the critical reading necessary to pick carefully through the staggering amount of information available today in print and digitally; and actively seek the wide, deep, and thoughtful engagement with high-quality literary and informational texts that builds knowledge, enlarges experience, and broadens worldviews. (NGA & CCSSO, 2010b, p. 3)

As an example of how a quest can bloom from a standard, consider this standard from eighth-grade civics: "Explain the powers and limits of the three branches of government, public officials, and bureaucracies at different levels in the United States and in other countries" (National Council for the Social Studies, 2013, p. 32). Students and their teacher explicitly describe what the standard's intended outcome is. With a common interpretation, they begin thinking about inquiry, game, and network design choices and determining what questions they need to ask. Then, they refine those questions with others like the following to get to the heart of the learning.

* What are the different levels of bureaucracies at the local level?
* In what capacities do those bureaucracies represent their constituents?
* What do local bureaucracies look like in other countries?

In the beginning phase, the questions are likely to be broader. You will refine them with continued coaching and conversation. Network design decisions might include, at the onset, what resources are physically close, then expanding with students' needs and objectives. Game design decisions might begin with modeling or mapping out how a legal action moves from an idea into the system to become a law.

Standards do not limit what educators teach, and they do not articulate how educators teach. Standards provide the minimums—non-negotiables—that teachers can use as quest inspiration. Teachers and students may want to focus on just one or two depending on time, interest, and depth of learning associated with one standard, or focus on all three as they learn a bundle of related standards that might demand a bigger or more sophisticated product or learning demonstration.

## Curriculum-Unit Maps

Schools organize curricula into topics that ideally describe core knowledge, key concepts, and learning targets. The curriculum content is a means to an end. If someone is teaching the history behind World War II, the goal is twofold: (1) a better understanding of conflict and (2) a better way of examining texts and associated media to seek patterns and make predictions. If the curriculum maps are clear on the *what* and the *why*, teachers can invite students to design potential quests. For instance, look at the curriculum-unit map for an elementary mathematics unit in figure 6.2.

| Content | Skills |
|---|---|
| ✧ Shapes<br>✧ Defining and nondefining attributes<br>✧ Two-dimensional and three-dimensional shapes<br>✧ Shape decomposition into two and four equal shares | ✧ Identify basic shapes using correct mathematics terminology.<br>✧ Describe, orally and through writing or drawing, the difference between defining and nondefining attributes.<br>✧ Draw, build, and share shapes with defining and nondefining attributes.<br>✧ Draw, build, and share two-dimensional and three-dimensional shapes.<br>✧ Decompose circles and rectangles into two and four equal shares.<br>✧ Compose circles and rectangles using two and four equal shares. |
| **Assessments** ||
| ✧ Preassessment: Read and discuss the book *Shapes*.<br>✧ Identify a variety of shapes. (Assessment is made through observation, consultation, manipulatives, or device play.)<br>✧ Given an attribute, draw shapes that match. Add nondefining attributes such as size, color, and orientation.<br>✧ Compose and decompose shapes using manipulatives, websites, or device applications. ||

Note: This content and these skills and assessments align to generalized standards and teachers can align them to specific standards.

*Source: Adapted from Fisher, 2015.*

Figure 6.2: Sample elementary curriculum-unit map.

In a first-grade unit on geometry basics, the teacher expects students to learn about shapes and their attributes as well as be able to deconstruct circles and rectangles into equal shares such as halves and fourths. In an already-documented unit, a teacher would define the instructional activities to engage students in developing the skills they need to deeply understand conceptual knowledge of shapes, knowing that this foundational knowledge is critical for understanding content in later grade levels, such as fractions and equations associated with formulas for perimeter, area, and volume. The teacher assesses students who have learned about shapes in the original unit on their ability to demonstrate understanding; during the assessment, students identify shapes, draw them, use mathematics manipulatives to create composite shapes, and deconstruct shapes into their component halves and fourths.

When questing, the assessment becomes a focal point in this curriculum-unit plan. If the assessment parameters just described are more formative as preparation for a larger, more unique assessment, then teachers can get to the heart of a questing experience even with students as early as first grade.

Invite students into this by asking where in their environment they see these shapes and how they can document their occurrence. Perhaps creating a shape exhibition that turns their classroom into a museum will interest students. Students can be responsible for taking pictures or shooting video and designing individual or group exhibits that represent shapes in their environment. The exhibit can include additional information about shapes (including defining and nondefining attributes), speculation on why the student included that shape in the environment, and information on how the student can deconstruct the shape into smaller shapes to demonstrate a basic fraction understanding. Other students in the school can visit this shape museum while the students who created the exhibits can be docents, explaining to others what they learned.

## Textbooks

Textbooks are doorways into content areas and represent clear positions of bias or thinking at a specific moment in time (Anyon, 1979; Apple & Christian-Smith, 1991; Ferguson, Brown, & Torres, 2016). Students can compare their texts to books from ages past or to contemporary thinking found in digital versions. They can compare them to textbooks of different cultures, regions, times, or purposes. Finally, textbooks are sources of sources. That is, textbooks have vetted sources and can launch a questing adventure just by opening doorways to primary sources, people to interview, and networks just waiting to be tapped. They can also provide a gateway of foundational knowledge that students can apply in authentic or unique circumstances, particularly if they relate to real-world events that would invite further study or questions.

For instance, across several grade levels, science texts task students with objectives related to plate tectonics, earthquakes, volcanoes, and other seismological content. Basic and content-specific vocabulary abound. What the textbook doesn't provide is real-world happenings that allow students to further explore, learn, investigate, analyze, and evaluate. Certainly, earthquakes and volcanic eruptions happen regularly enough that students could quest for various seismological and analytical tools for measuring and reporting tectonic shifts. They could quest about relatively new concepts such as fracking to extend their conceptual knowledge and provide opportunities to investigate those results in public-service presentations for those fracking impacts. This can extend to local university connections or earth science–related companies that might invite students to work alongside researchers.

If teachers and students see textbooks as a beginning rather than an end, the quest's trajectory lies in the potential questions that spring from the foundational concepts. Teachers and students can pose and pursue the following questions.

* What else do we need to know about earthquakes to understand the relationship between them and fracking?
* What impacts did the Indian Ocean earthquake and subsequent tsunami in 2004 have on the environment and the local economy?
* What, if any, warning systems or continued monitoring has been put into place in the wake of a large tectonic event like the 2004 Indian Ocean tsunami, the Sendai earthquake in Japan in 2011, or Eyjafjallajökull's volcanic eruption in Iceland in 2010?

## School Mission Statements or Themes

Schooling's broader aims are good for starting quests. Many schools have mission statements that clarify their commitment to learning and the learner. Take a look at an inspirational school mission statement from Avenues New York (n.d.):

> We will graduate students who are accomplished in the academic skills one would expect; at ease beyond their borders; truly fluent in a second language; good writers and speakers one and all; confident because they excel in a particular passion; artists no matter their field; practical in the ways of the world; emotionally unafraid and physically fit; humble about their gifts and generous of spirit; trustworthy; aware that their behavior makes a difference in our ecosystem; great leaders when they can be, good followers when they should be; on their way to well-chosen higher education; and, most importantly, architects of lives that transcend the ordinary.

This is fertile ground for ideas. "Aware that their behavior makes a difference in our ecosystem" can inspire the design of driving questions on areas such as how to reduce carbon emissions and how to be an informed and effective shopper (Avenues New York, n.d.). "Good writers and speakers" can inspire the investigation of narrative structure in social issue games in order to create and pitch an idea for a new game: a story that is highly adaptable based on the players' interaction and also follows a linear structure (Avenues New York, n.d.).

Magnet and charter schools often have themes associated with their design or mission, such as *environmental engineering* and *architecture*. Schools with these kinds of themes often approach them through curriculum design and ask teachers to create interdisciplinary units that address or include the theme. For example, Vista Innovation and Design Academy's (n.d.) values include "G: Grit to persevere; I: Innovating through design; L: Learning about empathy; Leading with integrity; S: Sparking creativity." Students in this school first understand a given problem through inquiry and research, as well as consultations within various network spaces. Past study topics at Vista Innovation and Design Academy include entrepreneurship, computer technologies, wellness, sculpture, biomimicry, graphic novels, and rocketry. Students synthesized information and imagined design possibilities.

## Current Events

Elevating student awareness of local and global issues is increasingly important as the world becomes more interdependent. Continued exposure to and analysis of economy, politics, social structures, and environment help students make better decisions about how to live their own lives now and in the future. The topics and issues that fascinate adults may also intrigue students, especially if they are broadly framed, like the following.

* **Students can examine the refugee crisis from multiple approaches, like legal protections, humanitarian aid, the handling of combatants, and mass exodus:** They should focus on different regions (Syria, Somalia, and Myanmar, for example), exploring diverse texts (photographs, investigative journalism, and United Nations policy) and points of view. They can visit the online newspaper map (www.newspapermap.com) for thousands of global online newspapers in different languages.

* **Students can investigate the challenges, policy considerations, and safety precautions that self-driving cars pose:** Self-driving cars are undergoing active tests on highways and city streets. The issues students investigate require development before anyone can purchase these cars. Students can pursue this topic from a variety of angles, like making the car affordable for the average consumer, uncovering the legality of who the driver is (a computer or a person), preventing hackers from taking over the car's computer functions, or assessing how self-driving cars function in severe weather conditions.

* **Students can study the decline in full-time reporters and photojournalists and its impact on publications as smartphones and other technological developments now make anyone a journalist:** Many people have become budding journalists, archiving an event, injustice, or experience in real time for the world to see. As more people snap pictures, take videos, and provide commentary, the ways in which new and old media tell stories and maintain audience interest have shifted. Students can learn what it takes for something to go viral and how to create stories through film and written text; and they can examine social media's impact on print, web-based, and television news organizations.

* **Students can investigate constitutional amendments and judicial law to determine when their rights are being violated:** Some students insist their constitutional rights are being violated. From locker searches to speech limiting, what rights and protections do citizens have? How does that change when students are in school? How does that change when someone is a minor?

They can play the video game *Do I Have a Right?* (www.gamesforchange
.org/play/do-i-have-a-right) to figure out how to help clients who believe their
rights have been violated. They can propose or make a case for a constitutional
amendment that repairs an injustice or clarifies parameters the founding
fathers could not envision (congressional term limits, a balanced budget,
birthplace and citizenship requirements to run for president, or equal rights,
for example) and then defend or dispute the amendment proposal. Students
can access the Constitutional Rights: Origins and Travels (n.d.) interactive
web tool "Explore Rights Around the World" (http://bit.ly/1hbJFVG) to
compare the U.S. Constitution to other countries' and determine how the
aforementioned scenarios would look under one of those country's laws.

Asking students what they know about the world is a good entry to topics relating to
current events.

## Challenge Clarification

After an initial idea, the next step is to frame the challenge. Teachers can do this in
classrooms by identifying learning goals (the *why* and the *what*) and the learning demonstration by way of a final product (the *deliverable*). Make space for something vibrant,
reinvigorate something stale, or run the challenge through the following criteria, which
Heidi Hayes Jacobs and Marie Alcock's (2017) work inspired. The question, problem,
challenge, topic, or issue should do the following.

* **Genuinely perplex the learner:** There is a compelling need or reason to figure
  it out.
* **Honor diverse perspectives:** There are multiple ways of framing an idea,
  approaching a challenge, or having respected points of view.
* **Include multiple disciplines:** There are natural connections among multiple
  subject areas; students make sense of a topic or challenge by leveraging relevant
  content and skills, regardless of its subject, to make the learning compelling.

See the online reproducible "Quest Decisions" for several guiding questions that you
can ask students in an effort to narrow or focus the challenge. (Visit **go.SolutionTree
.com/instruction** to download the reproducibles mentioned in this book.)

Perhaps a student still has difficulty thinking of a topic that grabs his or her interest
despite current events discussions and mission statement entry points. In those cases,
middle and high schoolers can frame the following quest challenges in various ways, but
here are a few illustrative examples in the form of hooking questions, as well as links to
provide background context or set the stage.

* **Do animals have feelings?** Start at BBC Earth Unplugged's (2013) video
  *Do Animals Have Feelings?—Earth Juice (Ep. 46)—Earth Unplugged*

(http://bit.ly/2q997Qa) and the TED Talk video *What Are Animals Thinking and Feeling?* (Safina, 2015; http://bit.ly/1I1DOPc).

* **What if people could be invisible or could fly?** Read Darren Orf's (2013) "8 Superpowers Brought to You by Technology" (http://bit.ly/2tu6YDj) to see how technology is helping close gaps between humans and superhumans.

* **What is work's future?** Read Keith Breene's (2016) piece "What Is the Future of Work?" (http://bit.ly/2r67Q0Z) for some information.

* **What are poverty's root causes?** Refer to the U.S. Conference of Catholic Bishops' (n.d.) directions for "The Stack of the Deck: An Illustration of the Root Causes of Poverty" (http://bit.ly/2pYDvl7), a game that illustrates this issue.

* **How do we get healthy foods into every community?** View the video at http://bit.ly/2rGoBvT to learn more.

* **What toys do children play with in different countries?** Students can compare their toys with those of other countries' children. Visit Dollar Street (Gapminder, n.d.; http://bit.ly/2sC43Wr) to answer this question.

* **How do we better understand the world and challenge our preconceived notions?** Check out Hans Rosling's (2006) TED Talk video (http://bit.ly/1kUuqgl) to watch him debunk myths about the "developing world." Then, see Gapminder (www.gapminder.org) to explore resources that use statistics to clarify misconceptions about global development.

## Learning Goals Mapping

After establishing the challenge, teachers can map learning goals to frame the questing experience. This *backward design* approach, which Grant Wiggins and Jay McTighe (1998) pioneered, offers stability to a fresh and potentially complex exploration of diverse topics.

As one example, figure 6.3 is a simplified version that articulates the challenge and related goals. The teacher takes the lead in drafting this version based on fluency with both the content and the standards.

| **Challenge:** Topic to explore framed as a hook, provocation, or question paired with a succinct explanation of what is at stake | |
| --- | --- |
| **Standard:** Excerpted from state, provincial, or national frameworks to demonstrate alignment | **Concept:** Big ideas to explore |
| | **Learning Target:** What student should know and be able to do as a result of the quest |

Figure 6.3: Learning goal map simplified.
*Visit **go.SolutionTree.com/instruction** for a free reproducible version of this figure.*

The second example (figure 6.4) uses *Understanding by Design* (Wiggins & McTighe, 2005) terminology to flesh out the learning goals: *long-term transfer goals, understandings and essential questions,* and *knowledge and skills.* We share both the simplified and the

*Understanding by Design* versions to make your transition into questing a bit easier (and do what is currently occurring in your school).

| Challenge: Topic to explore framed as a hook, provocation, or question paired with a succinct explanation of what is at stake | |
|---|---|
| Standard: Excerpted from state, provincial, or national frameworks to demonstrate alignment | Long-Term Transfer Goal: What student should be able to do independently as a result of being in school |
| | Understanding and Essential Questions: More developed big ideas, including—<br>✦ An understanding is an insight or generalization students need to uncover over the course of the quest.<br>✦ An essential question is written in student-friendly language to help them navigate through their questing journey—a tool to make sense of problems, challenges, texts, and experiences. |
| | Knowledge and Skill: What student should know and be able to do as a result of the quest |

*Source: Adapted from Wiggins & McTighe, 2005.*

Figure 6.4: Learning goal map with *Understanding by Design* terminology.
*Visit go.SolutionTree.com/instruction for a free reproducible version of this figure.*

With learning goals in place, you can begin thinking about deliverables.

## Deliverable Selection

After clarifying the challenge and mapping the learning goals, have students imagine the deliverable they would like to present at the end of the quest. The deliverable exhibits the student's expertise following the inquiries and exploration. You can consider the deliverable to be the final product or the journey's result. (The teacher assesses the deliverable; we discuss that in chapter 8, page 97.) With the teacher's help, students decide the parameters for the finished product. Parameters include the following.

* **Form:** A commercial pitch, mathematical model, game development, and so on
* **Criteria the teacher will consider to judge the work:** For example, inquiry criteria might be knowledge and understanding (content related to the inquiry), thinking (skills and processes), and application (proposed solution, conclusion, or further exploration)
* **Target audience:** Students in a classroom halfway around the world, virtual museumgoers, members of a particular online group, and so on

Revisiting the prompts at the beginning of chapter 7 (page 89) is incredibly helpful early on, but teachers and students will revisit these questions throughout a quest. Students will need to inevitably update or, potentially, reimagine these questions. Quests *can* deviate from their original plans as students uncover information that might lead them to a new question, a new network, or a new way to simulate or prototype what they are learning. Also revisit standards, learning targets, and big ideas to ensure that they align to the goals (which may need additions or deletions based on how the deliverable evolves). For example, if the topic is the ways in which screen time impacts how people connect with each other, a student might pursue the following deliverables.

* Create an FAQ (frequently asked *quest*ions) document to address consumer problems.
* Create a social media campaign to illustrate how connected and disconnected people feel.
* Develop a series of tutorials for senior citizens learning how to use technology.

Each deliverable has a different audience and purpose and should align with the curriculum topics specific to the form. At the same time, you relinquish some control for student choices. Here are authentic forms for several subject areas that have clear connections to both content standards and authentic audiences. Many of these forms can cross over to other subjects based on standards. For example, an interview could live in each category. World languages and English language arts could focus on the skills of posing questions and engaging in conversation during an interview. Science and visual and performing arts could focus on the topic in the content standards. The following lists provide deliverable ideas attached to particular content areas. Of course, these deliverable formats are not limited to these content areas.

Visual and performing arts:

* Curated art pieces (such as a portfolio or exhibition)
* Works (such as a sculpture or film)

World languages:

* Correspondence
* Itinerary
* Position statement on a regional or global issue
* Project proposal

Science:

* Data analysis
* Demonstration
* Investigative report
* Prototype

English language arts:

* Critique
* Editorial
* Interview
* Short story

Ideas for deliverable options will emerge throughout the quest as learners explore and connect. If the focus is constructing a viable argument and critiquing reasoning, many forms may measure that, including informational report, analysis, or persuasive statement. Within those broad forms, students can home in on specifics based on the challenge. For example, students may want to imagine an ideal playground that reflects priorities and special school community considerations (such as handicap accessibility, water sources, and natural materials). Students develop a play area within 1,200 feet of fencing and present that proposal to a panel of city planners for review. The written plan must include who the playground is designed for, dimensions and area for each play area within the playground, and why the planners should select the playground for construction.

As a generalized example, figure 6.5 offers an information graphic (or *infographic*) that can work as a potential new assessment form. The established criteria could be distilling students' research to a multimedia infographic representation.

*Source: Adapted from Creative Commons "Pack of four colorful infographic banners" by Freepik is licensed under CC0 1.0.*

Figure 6.5: Example infographic as deliverable.

When the audience changes, however, some planned deliverables may lead to unexpected outcomes that students prepare for with knowledge that they have gleaned from their work on the original deliverable. The following dialogue between a teacher and students shows how that might unfold.

| Ms. Martinez: | I'm so impressed with the short film that you made on students with asthma. I didn't realize the number of breathing triggers that were in our school. |
| Maria: | We didn't want to get anyone in trouble, like the teachers or anything, but everyone in our group has asthma, and we use our inhalers at school. Some of us were having problems in some classrooms. |
| Ms. Martinez: | I want you to know that during your research, I had a conversation with the principal and some other teachers. We agree with your concerns. In fact, the principal was so impressed with your film that she wants to show it at the next staff meeting, and we'd like you to present it to our board of education this month. |
| Mike: | Really? What about Mrs. Hardt and Coach Wilson? Won't they be mad that we're telling how much cologne they wear or sharing the number of class-rooms where the teachers use air fresheners? |
| Ms. Martinez: | Not at all. Those teachers had no idea that colognes and air fresheners could trigger an asthma attack. This is a great example of how research can lead to positive actions! The board will likely want you to speak about your film and your findings. |
| Maria: | We've got our script and the infographic we created. We could share that. |
| Mike: | We can make the script into a one- or two-page summary about what we found, share the infographic, and talk about good actions we can take. |
| Ms. Martinez: | I think that sounds like a fine plan. With your parents' permission, we'll add your film to our school's YouTube account as well. Perhaps you'll get even more ideas from commenters! |

In any quest, changing the target audience is acceptable if a student needs to realign learning targets or tweak the deliverable along the way, as long as the student is genuinely working toward his or her goals. It's unacceptable to change the audience or deliverable if the student is simply being indecisive. At some point, students must commit to their planned actions.

In terms of the potential quest, design, and deliverable choices, students and teachers may start out planning for a particular deliverable, but stay open to shifts (ambiguity) that lead to a different outcome.

## Sample Questing Thread

The disease sample quest has within it innumerable deliverable options for students in elementary, middle, and high schools. In this chapter, we group middle and high schools because possibilities are so similar.

### Elementary School

An elementary version might look something like what appears in figure 6.6.

**Challenge:** How can you better understand how diseases are spread? How can we inspire others to develop and maintain healthy practices that prevent the spread of disease? Your challenge is to help others understand healthy practices and how to prevent the spread of diseases through words and pictures.

**Standards:**

✧ Study "social interactions and group behavior" (3-LS-2); examine "interdependent relationships in ecosystems" (5-LS2-A; NGSS Lead States, 2013).

✧ "Comprehend concepts related to health promotion and disease prevention to enhance health" (CDC, 2016).

✧ "Inquire, think critically, and gain knowledge"; "draw conclusions, make informed decisions, apply knowledge to new situations, and create new knowledge" (American Association of School Librarians, 2007).

✧ "Analyze how two or more texts address similar themes or topics in order to build knowledge or to compare the approaches the authors take" (CCR.9; NGA & CCSSO, 2010b).

✧ "Synthesize and relate knowledge to personal experiences to make art"; "relate artistic ideas and works with societal, cultural, and historical context to deepen understanding" (National Coalition for Core Arts, 2012).

**Concepts:**

✧ Disease transmission

✧ Disease prevention

**Learning Targets:**

✧ Describe how diseases might spread among different types of organisms and what the diseases might do to a niche or ecosystem associated with those organisms.

✧ Experiment with and discover the way that some diseases might be spread.

✧ Seek out misconceptions or fears about the diseases and explain how you might relate the facts to those who misunderstand.

✧ Research and examine multiple types of media, including but not limited to the CDC and WHO briefings, photographs, news stories, interviews, and support groups appropriate for K–5 learners to learn about how diseases transmit and what we can do to prevent them.

✧ Draw conclusions based on synthesis of diverse types of media.

Figure 6.6: Simplified elementary learning goal map—disease quest.

Deliverables might look like those in figure 6.7 (page 84).

| Challenge | How can you better understand how diseases are spread? How can we inspire others to develop and maintain healthy practices that prevent the spread of disease? Your challenge is to use words and pictures to help others understand healthy practices and how to prevent the spread of diseases. |
|---|---|
| Potential Deliverables Imagined by Teacher and Students | ✦ Create a child-friendly guide to common diseases and their prevention.<br>✦ Orally or artistically present on common diseases for a younger audience or younger grade level.<br>✦ Digitally present with software like PowerPoint or a fee-based digital tool such as Canva (www.canva.com), Issuu (https://issuu.com), or LiveBinders (www.livebinders.com). (Teachers may need to prompt and support students at the elementary level.)<br>✦ Create a green screen video of students presenting in front of microscopic images, compelling images, or diagrams of prevention techniques. (Students at this level may need prompting and support.)<br>✦ Develop QR codes with unique content for other students to scan with their devices. |
| Potential Unexpected Outcomes | ✦ Partner with a museum for a digital layer of elementary school–produced content where museum visitors can also scan the QR codes and benefit from the students' work.<br>✦ If shared online, deliverables could go viral (pun intended), prompting additional conversations, defense of methodology by students, the asking and answering of questions, and so on. (Teachers may need parent permission for younger students. School administration or information technology directors will know the parameters of the Children's Internet Protection Act [2000] when sharing student work online.) |

Figure 6.7: Elementary deliverables and outcomes form—disease quest.

Again, quests are fluid, and these are simply examples of potential deliverables for elementary-level students, whose interests and ideas will differ.

## Middle School and High School

Figure 6.8 shows a secondary-level disease quest example using a simplified curriculum-unit template to articulate the challenge and goals of learning. Note that teachers would choose the standards for their grade level that relate to this challenge. Additionally, the deliverables and unexpected outcomes may vary depending on grade level, resources, and student contributions.

**Challenge:** How do you inspire a better understanding about what this disease is, how it spreads, and what actions we can take to slow down or stop it? Your challenge is to create a multidimensional picture of the disease using words, images, and data to humanize the devastation while also creating a level of urgency.

**Standards:**

✧ Study "growth, development, and reproduction of organisms" (MS-LS1-B); examine "inheritance and variation of traits" (HS-LS3-A-B; NGSS Lead States, 2013).

✧ "Comprehend concepts related to health promotion and disease prevention to enhance health" (CDC, 2016).

✧ "Inquire, think critically, and gain knowledge"; "draw conclusions, make informed decisions, apply knowledge to new situations, and create new knowledge" (American Association of School Librarians, 2007).

✧ "Analyze how two or more texts address similar themes or topics in order to build knowledge or to compare the approaches the authors take" (CCR.9; NGA & CCSSO, 2010a).

✧ "Synthesize and relate knowledge to personal experiences to make art"; "relate artistic ideas and works with societal, cultural, and historical context to deepen understanding" (National Coalition for Core Arts, 2012).

**Concepts:**

✧ Disease transmission

✧ Epidemic

✧ Empathy

**Learning Targets:**

✧ Describe the real impact of disease on families and relationships, specifically, emotional and financial toll and shifts in roles and responsibilities.

✧ Seek out misconceptions or fears about the disease, and explain the objective facts.

✧ Research and examine multiple types of texts, including but not limited to the CDC and WHO briefings, photographs, news stories, interviews, and support groups.

✧ Find and examine sources that identify the spread of the disease over time (past, present, and future predictions).

✧ Draw conclusions based on synthesis of a diverse set of texts.

✧ Create a compelling picture of the disease using illustrations and evidence.

Figure 6.8: Simplified secondary learning goal map—disease quest.

Figure 6.9 (page 86) uses a more sophisticated curriculum-unit template with which to map the disease quest (Wiggins & McTighe, 2005).

**Challenge:** How do you inspire a better understanding about what this disease is, how it spreads, and what actions we can take to slow down or stop it? Your challenge is to create a multidimensional picture of the disease using words, images, and data to humanize the devastation while also creating a level of urgency.

**Standards:**
- Study "growth, development, and reproduction of organisms" (MS-LS1-B); examine "inheritance and variation of traits" (HS-LS3-A-B; NGSS Lead States, 2013).
- "Comprehend concepts related to health promotion and disease prevention to enhance health" (CDC, 2016).
- "Inquire, think critically, and gain knowledge"; "draw conclusions, make informed decisions, apply knowledge to new situations, and create new knowledge" (American Association of School Librarians, 2007).
- "Analyze how two or more texts address similar themes or topics in order to build knowledge or to compare the approaches the authors take" (CCR.9; NGA & CCSSO, 2010b).
- "Synthesize and relate knowledge to personal experiences to make art"; "relate artistic ideas and works with societal, cultural, and historical context to deepen understanding" (National Coalition for Core Arts, 2012).

**Long-Term Transfer Goals:**
- Seek to investigate challenging contemporary global and local issues by pursuing questions or a line of thinking.
- Navigate through diverse sources and perspectives to make discerning and thoughtful judgments.
- Think flexibly, take responsible risks, and listen with understanding and empathy while engaging with the world.

**Understandings and Essential Questions:**
- *Disease transmission*—Reliable information about the urgency and severity of a disease has to be balanced with reliable information about how the disease spreads to generate public action. How do we prevent the spread of deadly diseases? At what cost?
- *Epidemic*—By comparing texts, readers often gain greater insight into those texts. How do I make sense of the information I find? What conclusions can I draw?
- *Empathy*—Empathy is feeling with people. How do I communicate information and ideas in order for people to become more connected?

**Knowledge and Skills:**
- Describe the real impact of disease on families and relationships, specifically, emotional and financial toll and shifts in roles and responsibilities.
- Seek out misconceptions or fears about the disease and explain the objective facts.
- Research and examine multiple types of texts, including but not limited to the CDC and WHO briefings, photographs, news stories, interviews, and support groups.
- Find and examine sources that identify the spread of the disease over time (past, present, and future predictions).
- Draw conclusions based on synthesis of a diverse set of texts.
- Create a compelling picture of the disease using illustrations and evidence.

*Source: Adapted from Wiggins & McTighe, 2005.*

Figure 6.9: Secondary learning goal map—disease quest.

The example in figure 6.10 illustrates a potential unexpected outcome. Use this form with students throughout their journeys.

| Challenge | How do you inspire a better understanding about what this disease is, how it spreads, and what actions we can take to slow down or stop it? Your challenge is to create a multidimensional picture of the disease using words, images, and data to humanize the devastation while also creating a level of urgency. |
|---|---|
| **Potential Deliverables Imagined by Teacher and Students** | ✧ Report<br>✧ Rhetorical speech<br>✧ Digital presentation with software like PowerPoint or a fee-based digital tool such as Canva (www.canva.com), Issuu (https://issuu.com), or LiveBinders (www.livebinders.com).<br>✧ Infographics<br>✧ Filmed commercial or documentary<br>✧ Frequently asked questions about diseases for the community<br>✧ Mathematical modeling of a disease outbreak |
| **Potential Unexpected Outcomes** | ✧ Present to the CDC on research findings<br>✧ If shared online, potential for deliverables to go viral (pun intended), prompting additional conversations, defense of methodology by students, the asking and answering of questions, and so on<br>✧ More involvement in a loved one's medical care and treatment decisions when he or she is dealing with a disease |

*Source: Adapted from Wiggins & McTighe, 2005.*

Figure 6.10: Secondary deliverables and outcomes form—disease quest.

*Visit **go.SolutionTree.com/instruction** for a free reproducible version of this figure.*

# Coda

While questing may be unfamiliar, this chapter sought inspiration from touchstones familiar to every teacher to launch a quest, namely: standards, curriculum-unit maps, school mission statements, current events, and students themselves. The teacher coaches students to consider the challenge (curriculum content), learning targets (aligned with standards), and deliverable ideas (summative assessment).

As you start opening up space for students so you can design with then, in tandem, you tap into their inventiveness, imagination, and aspirations. This is more of a learning partnership than a hierarchy, driven by a shared desire to make learning relevant, rigorous, and interesting.

# CHAPTER 7

# Introducing Students to Quests

This chapter and chapter 8 (page 97) provide instructional guidance for operationalizing the quest with your students. In this chapter, which gamification and behavioral design expert Yu-kai Chou's (n.d.) discovery and onboarding stages of gaming inspired, we take you through the process of introducing students to quests, including:

* Grabbing students' attention and letting them discover
* Onboarding with curriculum for ramping up students' knowledge about upcoming quests
* Helping students with design choices

These decisions create crucial emotional connections to the learning. Personal support and excitement building are part of the focus. Spending time and attention on the *why* and *how* we think and work together when you are co-designing quests increases the likelihood that students will want to take action.

## Discovery

Students require a hook to catch their interest. For example, a teacher might set up artifacts like models, learning stations, or previous student work; read a compelling story; or play a video clip that leaves students wondering what happens next. This piques learners' interest, hooking them. It is important to note that during the hook, students do not yet know what they are learning about. They are not reading directions or engaging with material. Consider the disease quest example. The challenge is to create a multidimensional picture of disease using words, images, and data.

Consider introductions that can trigger big ideas from students. In the disease quest, that might include disease transmission, epidemics, or empathy. Propose something that will capture attention and trigger a toward state through emotion and interest. Again, *toward states* occur when the brain perceives or classifies an event as good; students want to move toward something when they are in this state (Davachi et al., 2010). For example, the following are various challenges to launch discovery about the topic of disease.

* Find pictures of the human body that show the ravages of one of the world's deadliest epidemics, and ask students, "How did this happen?"
* Direct the class to play the board game *Pandemic* without any introduction.
* Provide a CDC botulism case study for students to investigate.
* "Quarantine" the classroom or section of school, and then explain the rules of a quarantine to help students see both the harshness and the reasoning behind the segregation.
* Show a clip from any pandemic movie, and stop it when characters begin to panic.
* Enlarge an image of a virus that is either beautiful or terrifying, and ask for reactions. Ask students, "Who am I?" Or, offer in a menacing tone, "Know your enemy" or "Take me to your leader."
* Dress up in a germ costume, or present a germ puppet, and tell a story.

Avoid deep debriefs. Make no direct instruction. Spend little time on whole-class reflection. A student just introduced to a quest topic is unlikely to identify targets or truly learn material. He or she is simply discovering. If metacognition comes into play, and the student is aware of his or her own thinking, he or she may wonder why he or she wants or needs to learn about a topic. And while instructional time is incredibly precious, teachers cannot expedite or remove the discovery experience in favor of starting work. How attentive students are, how visceral their responses are, and their imagining possibilities are worthwhile investments.

For example, a teacher's unit plan describes the learning opportunities that will take place as students begin learning about the Underground Railroad. Instructional activities might include a video to hook them in and text to read about it. During the video, which is the hook, students become interested and ask questions about the Underground Railroad and the people associated with it. The teacher could continue his or her currently documented plan, or take advantage of student interest and launch a quest that goes well beyond what he or she originally planned.

Once they're hooked, the next phase is onboarding.

## Onboarding

*Onboarding* is when teachers "train the users to become familiar with the rules of the game, the options, the mechanics, and the win-states" (Chou, n.d.). This training takes place through the development of a *student-facing curriculum*, a joint commitment where teachers and students have responsibility and direction for their pursuits.

In this curriculum, the teacher is accountable for the following.

* Drafting short-term and long-term targets that align with relevant content standards

* Describing learning targets in language that
* Sharing the complete view where they see ho
  to the long-term goals

Students are accountable for the following.

* Clarifying the full story by asking questions,
* Imagining and exploring based on the compl
  related learning targets
* Learning how to lead the way (instead of the

Student-facing curriculum grows positive experienc
students navigate design choices on how to approach process and deliverables. When
students complete a learning goal map, they are participating in curriculum co-creation
and ensuring accessible learning targets by creating both short- and long-term goals.

## Curriculum Co-Creation

As part of the onboarding stage, teachers have students fill out the learning goal map in
figure 7.1. Prior to this, the teacher completes either a simplified learning goal map (see
figure 6.3, page 78) or an *Understanding by Design*–inspired learning goal map (see figure
6.4, page 79; Wiggins & McTighe, 2012). The teacher immediately follows by having
students get to work on the unit. The student can build additional targets and expectations for his or her version of the quest. The version in figure 7.1 is that of a high school
student who is onboarding for the disease quest. Helping students create this learning
goal map is the key to creating the invitation for co-creation in the classroom and clearly
communicating the quest plan and minimum requirements.

| Challenge: Figure out what this disease is, how it spreads, and what actions we can take to slow down or stop it. Create a powerful way to communicate that message to your audience, making sure that people take this seriously, but also try to show care and compassion for those who are sick or dead. | |
|---|---|
| **Essential Questions:** | **Long-Term Goals:** |
| ✧ How do we prevent the spread of deadly diseases? At what cost? <br> ✧ How do I make sense of the information I find? What conclusions can I draw? <br> ✧ How do I communicate information and ideas in order for people to become more connected? | ✧ I can investigate a challenging contemporary global or local issue. <br> ✧ I can use diverse sources and points of view to figure out what happened, what's true, and what's a reasonable conclusion. <br> ✧ I can step back from an idea or problem and figure out or consider another way. <br> ✧ I can listen to others' points of view, information, and ideas to reflect on how that might shape what to do next. |

Figure 7.1: Learning goal map—student version.

continued ➧

92 THE QUEST FOR LEARN

Student-Driven
✧ How does
✧ What is
   onese
✧ If

| Questions: | Short-Term Learning Targets: |
|---|---|
| ◌ person get malaria? ◌he best way to protect ◌f and others from malaria? ◌alaria was discovered in 1800, why is there still no vaccine? | ✧ I can describe the disease's real impact on families and relationships. ✧ I can seek out misconceptions or fears about the disease and explain objective facts. ✧ I can research and examine multiple types of texts to determine what's accurate. ✧ I can find and examine sources that identify the spread of the disease over time (past, present, and future predictions). ✧ I can draw conclusions based on the information I find. ✧ I can create a compelling picture of the disease using illustrations and evidence. |

Visit **go.SolutionTree.com/instruction** for a free reproducible version of this figure.

A student is essentially filling out a kind of user profile and beginning a commitment when completing this learning goal map. Ideally, the student documents the process. Based on our observations, many students already do this in some form—writing important information in a student planner (teacher initiated) or making a bulleted list of achievement steps or a timeline of goals (student initiated). We advocate for a student-created document that is more intentional than what students (or their teachers) have previously documented.

Teachers may ask students to discuss or record what they anticipate learning and an idea for their deliverable. They may brainstorm how they get to their deliverable with questions such as the following.

* Do I need to learn how to write an argument? How do I write an argument? How do I make sure I have a claim, a counterclaim, and supporting details?
* How do arguments connect to the topic or question I am exploring?
* Where could I show that I know how to write an argument while making a connection or contribution to my topic of choice?
* Whom do I need to network with to make a valid, high-quality, and worthy argument? Will it be fun? Who will give me feedback, and what will that feedback look like?
* What can my teacher do to support me? Do I need anyone else to help me? Who else would be interested in my idea besides my teacher?

## Accessible Learning Targets: Long Term and Short Term

The student-facing learning goal map includes long-term goals and short-term learning targets that represent opportunities for students to reach the win state. The student can document a series of small wins, or short-term learning targets, as he or she works toward long-term quest goals and deliverables.

Organize learning targets that align to the curriculum standards, and translate them for students. Typically, the teacher does this prior to students filling out the learning plan. For example, the standard might be, "Write arguments to support claims with clear reasons and relevant evidence" (W.6.1; NGA & CCSSO, 2010a). Together, you may need to break down that standard into several learning targets like the following.

* I can find and use credible evidence to support my claims.
* I can organize each of my claims and supporting details or evidence to help the reader understand my logic.
* I can use words and phrases to clarify how the supporting details or evidence connect to the claim.

If a student does not understand the target, he or she cannot co-create a learning experience. When you speak openly with students about the plan and expectations, the student is able to contribute without risking a gap in his or her learning or doing it wrong.

Ask students to consider what the long-term goals are and to explicitly define *We can* statements. They might look like the following *We can* statements.

* **Writing:** We can use descriptive details to show what we mean.
* **Research skills:** We can locate and read information to help better understand a topic.
* **Problem solving:** We can break a problem into smaller parts to solve it.
* **Collaboration:** We can use individuals' expertise and knowledge to accomplish a goal.

In the disease quest example, *We can* statements also specify either the content a quester must learn or his or her interests.

* We can work professionally with the CDC as a valued member of our affinity space.
* We can contribute to member and mentor spaces that would benefit from our collective learning about diseases. (This is a potential zone for an unexpected outcome or unplanned extension of the deliverable as well.)

This thinking emphasizes collaboration. *We can* statements facilitate students co-designing specific facets of the collaborative work. These concepts help students stay attentive to how their learning situates among their peers or network members. For instance, a student participating in a member space might learn something that impacts his or her quest's path or deliverable. In turn, the deliverables, particularly if they are shared back to network spaces, might provide answers that future student questers need. That moves the students from a member space participant to a potential expert in a mentor space.

## Design Choices

The final aspect of introducing students to quests is to talk design. All quests leverage choices in question, game, and network designs. The following sections speak to the question, game, and network design choices students and teachers must address together when using the design elements.

### Question Design Choices

After the teacher ensures the learning targets are clear, the next step is for students to pose questions that plan their learning experience. Students begin to design questions based on ideas triggered from the discovery phase, initial ideas, or both as they are navigating the onboarding phase. You may have to host a series of lessons on question crafting, evaluating, and refining. (See Eileen Depka's [2017] *Raising the Rigor: Effective Questioning Strategies and Techniques for the Classroom* for help.)

Examine the initial student-driven questions from the previous disease quest example on malaria (figure 7.1, page 91). Figure 7.2 shows the kind of assessment a teacher might provide. The teacher's feedback goes back to the student, which increases the student's understanding of the actionable, open-ended questions that the student believes are worth pursuing.

| Student-Driven Question | Question Evaluation |
|---|---|
| How does a person get malaria? | This is a closed question with a straightforward answer. It can become more open if we explore treatment after infection. |
| What is the best way to protect oneself and others from malaria? | This is a more open question, especially because there are suggestions to prevent a mosquito bite but no fail-safe recommendations. |
| If malaria was discovered in 1800, why is there still no vaccine? | This question can go in very different directions. You could spend time looking at current research for a vaccine. Or you could research and identify where malaria is most prevalent and implications of it being a regional, not worldwide, concern. Another interesting idea might be researching other mosquito bite–transmitted diseases (like yellow fever, Zika virus, and Japanese encephalitis). |

Figure 7.2: Teacher assessment of students' driving questions.

As the questions and design challenges evolve and deepen, the teacher and student will need to revisit the long-term goals, learning targets, and related standards to ensure that they align. For example, when students are taking on an engineering challenge, the learning targets might focus on gathering information and listening with empathy to articulate the users' concerns; developing a prototype; and testing prototypes by their ability to achieve the objective and address user feedback.

The focus is on the overall goal and getting the student to articulate his or her thinking.

## Game Design Choices

Game design hinges on whether a learner will play or design a game. Game design can be as small as a die element in an activity or as large as an online gaming environment with a complete wiki affinity space. Teachers and students should begin where they are comfortable but be ready and willing to accept evolution.

When students do choose game design elements, it is helpful for teachers to play. Play the games, play similar games, and model appreciating their beauty and the joy of playing them to learn. Doing so brings this part of the framework to life in the classroom. When facilitating this section of the quest, present criteria for limits and include samples that students can use as models. Limits might include only board games if students do not have access to electronic devices in the classroom. Another limit might be game time; a teacher may suggest only games that can be played in two hours or less, which excludes lots of games (some of which can take over twenty—or even over one hundred—hours to complete). When you introduce a limit, suggest samples within the limits. It will help students make appropriate choices.

Because game design elements include playing similar games and modeling, there's the potential for a lot of topic-related research that would enable a student to modify an off-the-shelf game, while simultaneously maintaining the game's inner structure and player roles. For example, modifying just parts of *Pandemic* for the disease quest allows two different layers of learning to happen concurrently: (1) the student has to learn about what diseases do, how they behave, ways they spread, and how they impact populations and (2) the student imagines and creates new scenarios related to malaria, which requires research and game play. In turn, he or she may discover information that results in the agreed-on deliverable (in this case, a modified version of *Pandemic*). Students could also potentially use *Pandemic*'s expansions as models because they contain newer scenarios and additional roles for students. These additional roles are particularly helpful if cooperative groups have more than four students (which is the maximum number of players for *Pandemic* off the shelf).

## Network Design Choices

All questers require networks whether they are employing network design or not. After posing initial questions and ensuring learning target comprehension, it is time for students to choose the networks they will use. Because they may not know much about the different network types or how to leverage them for learning, it is critical for teachers to both model and facilitate this process so it is safe, effective, and ethical, as described in chapter 5 (page 51). Modeling how to use learning networks and frequently connecting to them as a class can help students think creatively about their own questing experiences and make quality choices in this area.

When students are digging into a topic and interpreting the instruction in relation to networking choices, it might be helpful to go back to a series of questions that appear in chapter 5 (see page 59), a few of which follow.

* Who has the information we need?
* Who knows more about this?
* How do we manage misinformation?
* Who needs our information?
* What networks should we start reaching out to?

## Coda

This chapter focused on capturing student attention and interest through the discovery, onboarding, and design phases. The discovery phase hooks students and triggers emotional responses. The discovery experience is a necessary part of quest introduction. Instructional time is incredibly precious, but remember that the quality of attention, the emotional responses, and the prediction of what can happen are worth that time.

The discovery phase immediately leads into the onboarding phase, where you officially invite students to co-create the questing curriculum. Once students are aware of the required learning targets, you can include them in the process as self-directed learners. The entire quest's plan is really launched right here. The design will evolve, but the initial shared vision launches the process.

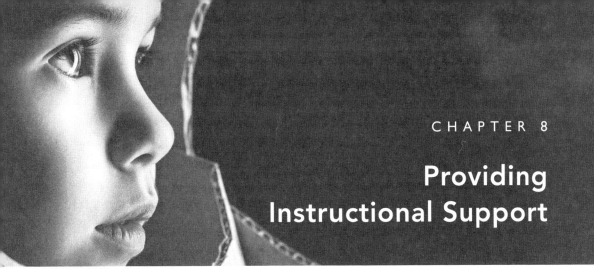

# CHAPTER 8

# Providing Instructional Support

How does a teacher support his or her learners throughout a quest? Once it is underway, what kind of support does he or she offer? What conversations are necessary about the plans or deviations from them? This chapter focuses on how a teacher supports learners throughout a quest: the delicate balancing act between support and self-direction, which aligns with Chou's (n.d.) scaffolding in stages of gaming. *Scaffolding* refers to a variety of instructional supports that move students progressively toward greater independence in the learning process. However, if students do not know its purpose, they can easily become dependent on the teacher to decide how to approach an assignment, process, or text.

During a quest, scaffolding helps students practice, see the impact of their actions, and seek out resources. They show commitment to learning. For an example, look back at decisions five through nine in figure 6.1 (page 68). That is where this chapter focuses—a detailed explanation of the timeline and action plan, commitment statements, checkpoints, formative assessment design, and feedback.

## Timeline and Action Plan

Questing, though more open ended than certain pedagogies, does live within limits. Creating a timeline keeps the quest's scope and scale within the bounds of the given schedule for students early on so steps are realistic. Figure 8.1 (page 98) is one such example. To avoid a step-by-step, formulaic approach, this part is co-created with students and is limited only by your creativity.

The student timeline and action plan are critical for (1) structuring a quester's steps and (2) letting students practice skills without fearing scores or evaluation. Use the form with students when they organize their approach, but keep in mind that they can adjust their action plans midquest. It also makes perfect sense to have different documents for different quest designs so they align to the choices students will make in those experiences. Students also can use this kind of logistical tool as a journal during a quest, revisiting and revising it; as an additional reflection tool; or as evidence of the process.

| Action Plan | | | | |
|---|---|---|---|---|
| Task | Person Responsible | Learning Target | Materials Needed | Time Needed |
| Play Friv games to explore information. | | | | Five days |
| Read the butterfly books. | | | | Three days |
| Draw a life cycle. | | | | One hour |
| Talk to Mr. Leonard in the library. | | | | One hour |

Figure 8.1: Student timeline and action plan example.

*Visit **go.SolutionTree.com/instruction** for a free reproducible version of this figure.*

When questing is new to either teacher or student, it can be helpful to have digital forms available in a learning management system or to keep the forms in a folder or binder in the classroom. Teachers and students who are comfortable with questing can think of these documents as the learners' tools. They should allow them to demonstrate increasing levels of self-direction. Students may even create their own versions, customized to the topic that interests them.

## Commitment Statement

The commitment statement is a tool that inspires learners to create high-quality work. Questing takes effort. Being accountable for their self-direction is a crucial 21st century skill (Jacobs & Alcock, 2017; Partnership for 21st Century Learning, n.d.). Because the learner will co-create the quest and make decisions during it, a commitment statement like the one in figure 8.2 can empower the learner to apply him- or herself to the quest. Research shows that signing such a statement can help students follow through on the work (Kotler & Lee, 2008).

I work hard on tough questions. I focus on my learning needs. I consider many choices and make my selections. I commit to learning more about _____. The results of this quest help make me a stronger communicator and social change agent.

Name: _____    Date: _____

*Source: Adapted from Klein, 2009.*

Figure 8.2: Sample individual commitment statement.

*Visit **go.SolutionTree.com/instruction** for a free reproducible version of this figure.*

Whereas figure 8.2 exemplifies a commitment statement that an individual student might adhere to, the statement in figure 8.3 exemplifies a group's commitment and would work for collaborative teams.

We use the design, learn possible solutions, try ideas, and decide what will become the solution. We expect our initial design to change as we become experts and look forward to presenting our deliverable by _____. We will archive our journey so we can move forward with refinements and revisions.

Names: _____    Date: _____

*Source: Adapted from Klein, 2009.*

Figure 8.3: Sample team commitment statement.
*Visit **go.SolutionTree.com/instruction** for a free reproducible version of this figure.*

Do not be surprised if students push back against this commitment; they exert much less intellectual energy when they sit through a lecture or are told exactly what and how to learn. It is helpful to revisit the commitment statement after each conference or interview with the learner during the quest, and it is important for students to routinely reflect on their roles as learners and designers throughout the quest. They can recommit, return to the design, and change elements if needed for better learning.

Consider the following probing question frames and stems when working with a quester.

* Tell me, how is your work in this area going? Is it getting easier to do this part? If not, why do you think that is? If yes, what have you been doing that is working?
* Are you still interested in learning more about this? Why or why not?
* Have you gotten any feedback that was particularly helpful? What did you choose to keep? Did you decide to change anything yet?
* Do you believe you can complete this on schedule? What can you adjust to stay on schedule?
* Do you want to consider changing the driving question to fit what you have learned now? What will you do if that happens?
* What will you do next? What can you do right away?
* What do you need from us to help you be successful? What do you still need to learn to make this work?

Checkpoints and meetings midquest help both student and teacher. They're explained next.

## Checkpoints

Since quests, by design, are open ended and could potentially change direction, teachers need opportunities to check student progress. These checkpoints can be examinations for understanding or conferences and allow teachers to redirect misconceptions with content knowledge, point out flawed logic, identify biased resources, correct off-track wanderings, and address disengagement.

Checkpoints also serve as milestones on the road to the deliverable. In addition to establishing or revising important dates for completion, they can mimic professional language. How would someone in the profession approach that challenge? Each column in figure 8.4 documents the progress for a deliverable—making a game, making a television show, and making a website—by phase. Students research and learn steps for creating products in these media and use expert parlance to list those major steps, which serve as checkpoints along the way.

| Making a Game | Making a Television Show | Making a Website |
|---|---|---|
| 1. Concept<br>2. Research<br>3. Integration (big pieces of the design)<br>4. Prototype (design layout)<br>5. Draft rules<br>6. Game development<br>7. Beta testing<br>8. Editing<br>9. Production<br>10. Feedback and versioning | 1. Pitching<br>2. Noting<br>3. Outlining<br>4. Scripting<br>5. Casting<br>6. Filming<br>7. Upfronting<br>8. Staffing | 1. Information gathering<br>2. Planning<br>3. Designing<br>4. Developing<br>5. Testing and delivery<br>6. Maintaining |

Figure 8.4: Sample deliverables by checkpoint.

Consider checkpoint scheduling and affinity space–member connections to optimize the feedback opportunities. Students can complete checkpoints with classmates, teachers, or affinity space members who are willing to support them.

## Formative Assessment Design

Because quests are fluid, organic experiences that often do not wait for a single summative event, formative assessments are the ideal tool with which to provide ongoing feedback to students. With these assessments, teachers can provide specific prescriptions for refinement, contributing to the learning cycle of expertise. The primary user of the formative assessment results is the learner who revisits the learning targets and, with the formative feedback, improves his or her performance.

Formative assessment provides two kinds of feedback.

1. How well the learner is doing toward meeting the stated targets (for example, how he or she is doing on the mathematics standards)
2. How the learner's strategies are working (for example, if working alone or working with a partner is best for learning the mathematics standards)

This is why formative assessments so effectively improve student performance (Black & Wiliam, 2009). Teachers who use them can produce observable and measurable results in classrooms that rival one-to-one tutoring. When structured correctly, formative assessments can teach students just as much about *how* they learn as they do about specific standards or topics. In addition, they help structure the process. That frees teachers from managing and directing a quest's every aspect, which affords learners the opportunity to direct progress; teachers do not have to relinquish monitoring and intervening or supporting learners when necessary.

Initial assessment, which requires forethought, and post-assessment plans, which ask students for next steps, are discussed next.

## Initial Assessment

Formative assessments are intentional, planned events. They are *front-end heavy*, which is to say a teacher must design the formative assessments and learning strategies prior to the unit and connect them to learning targets. The learner receives these things at the beginning of the learning process. Figure 8.5 is an initial formative assessment— a descriptive rubric.

| Learning Target | At Target | Approaching Target | Notes |
|---|---|---|---|
|  |  |  |  |
|  |  |  |  |
|  |  |  |  |

*Source: © Alcock, 2012.*

Figure 8.5: Formative assessment rubric—initial.

*Visit **go.SolutionTree.com/instruction** for a free reproducible version of this figure.*

Record the student's learning targets in the first column. Most of these learning targets will come from the curriculum, which in turn will often come from unpacked standards and then additional content knowledge or skills. Do not include every learning target from your curriculum. Instead, prioritize them to make things manageable.

During a quest, a student may identify additional content beyond the curriculum, which results in additional (or possibly the removal of) learning targets on his or her formative assessment. In the At Target and Approaching Target columns, indicate where the student is with *yes* or *no*, or place an *X* where appropriate. The data that inform this rubric can come from a selected-response test, essay, performance task, or personal communication—any form or method as defined in Robert J. Marzano's (2003) and Rick Stiggins and colleagues' (2007) work.

Give specific feedback in the Notes column such as, *Your introduction inspired me to do greater things* or *I placed a star on your written pitch where the introduction should be; I could not find it.* Keep the Notes portion of the assessment clean. You want to minimize the time it takes to complete and process (for both yourself and the student). Because it is not an evaluative rubric that must have points or levels, you can home in on two critical elements: (1) Is the learner at the target? and (2) What specifically does the student need next—practice or new learning? These notes enable the student to process the feedback in the assessment reflection and make useful choices in the post-assessment plan.

## Assessment Reflection

From there, the student sorts the feedback into a graphic organizer for a sense of where he or she is in relation to mastering the targets. This graphic organizer appears in its simplest form in figure 8.6, where it separates the data into three parts. Quester feedback processing occurs here because the learner must have the opportunity to process received feedback; doing so helps the student self-regulate, or reflect and focus (Jacobs & Alcock, 2017). This reflection also confirms metacognition about where the learner is in his or her process.

| I know these: |
|---|
| I need to practice these: |
| I need to learn these: |

Figure 8.6: Quester feedback processing—reflection.

*Visit **go.SolutionTree.com/instruction** for a free reproducible version of this figure.*

The top section of the reflection—*I know these*—acknowledges what the student has learned already and signals to the brain what is desirable. This is vital to keep the learner in the toward state. The reflection then separates the constructive feedback into two groups: (1) things learners need to practice and (2) things they need to learn. This division helps make the student feel as if the unmet targets are manageable. It also lays out specific targets that need extra engagement. This challenges and then stimulates norepinephrine release in the brain because it provides a timeline for the learner, a timeline vital for student motivation (Davachi et al., 2010).

## Post-Assessment Plan

The subsequent formative assessment asks the learner to identify specific strategies he or she will use to improve on each target identified as needing practice or new learning in the reflection portion. The plan is organized by target and specific next steps and co-created with students. Figure 8.7 shows an example, but is only partially completed to avoid limiting your creativity.

| Learning Target | Possible Learning Strategy |
|---|---|
| I can clearly introduce my topic. | |
| I can organize my writing logically. | 1. Use this plan as a guide to plan for your own essay.<br>2. Examine this model plan filled out, and then follow it with your own materials.<br>3. Work with a friend to read this model essay; deconstruct the logical organization of the model and label each part of the essay.<br>4. Watch this video on how to organize an essay and then take notes.<br>5. Create your own learning strategy. |
| I can select relevant evidence. | |
| I can draw conclusions based on the information I find. | |
| I can research and examine multiple types of texts to determine what's accurate. | |
| I can find and examine sources that identify the spread of the disease and ways to prevent further spread. | |
| I can investigate a challenging contemporary global or local issue. | |
| I can explore and discover the way that some diseases might be spread. | |
| I can seek out misconceptions or fears about how disease spreads and provide accurate information. | |

*Source: © Alcock, 2016.*

Figure 8.7: Formative assessment with learning strategies—post-assessment plan.
*Visit **go.SolutionTree.com/instruction** for a free reproducible version of this figure.*

The next steps are examples based on the target and apply to different quests. Imagine some next steps for other learning targets with which your students must show mastery. The bottom of the learning plan includes a location for questers' commitment statement and a place to sign to allow students to show ownership. This will be part of the timeline that undergoes adjustment after each check-in.

When asking students for next steps, prepare to hear nonspecific replies such as, "I will work harder," "I will study more," and "I will reread the chapter." These strategies are too vague. Listing possible learning strategies by learning target facilitates learning target practice and allows enough time for students to try learning strategies and adjust if they are not getting the results they want. Thus, students get feedback on how well their learning strategy is working. We believe it is important to include the option for students to create their own strategy in the list to encourage students to think about the best way for them to learn the target.

The three-part formative assessment allows the gradual release of a curriculum's nonnegotiable learning targets into the learner's hands without constant check-ins. It increases the learner's independence. The result is one of self-regulation, self-assessment, and self-motivation to improve performance (Lambert et al., 2016).

## Feedback

The quester needs descriptive feedback to create and follow the learning plan. Think of feedback as an intertwined spiral of four iterative steps: (1) plan, (2) act, (3) examine, and (4) begin again. Combined and repeated, the first three steps provide structure for feedback and reflections. The last steps mean starting over again with the benefit of gained knowledge and feedback. The spiral can apply to any event or process, and the good news is that learners never return to the start in a spiral. They move forward, always progressing to a new place (Costa & Kallick, 1995). Figure 8.8 helps you visualize that spiral.

**Ongoing Feedback and Reflection**

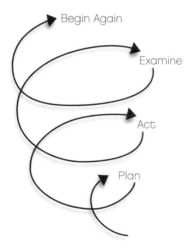

*Source: Adapted from Costa & Kallick, 1995.*

Figure 8.8: Feedback spiral.

The following sections describe each step in the feedback spiral.

## Plan

In planning, the learner decides what to focus on; the quester should clearly explain the whats and whys of his or her choice. Is it a new problem? Is it a facet of the work? Is it an unknown twist? Is it a created product? The teacher, mentor, expert, or peer helps guide the learner to his or her refined vision.

## Act

The learner takes action to reach the learning target, which may include skill practice, information research, experimentation, or exploration. When taking action, the person reflecting—in this case the quester—is pondering questions about his or her choices: Is it working? What problems, if any, have surfaced? Do I need to adjust anything? The results are small, tangible products or performances on the journey to the deliverable. Questers can collect these artifacts to document and reflect on their journey. The artifacts may or may not actually be part of the deliverable, but they are evidence of the process.

## Examine

After taking action, the learner pauses to use feedback to examine what happened. Reflecting is usually in response to feedback, more focused questions, an unintended result, or an unexpected event. Ideally, students are habitual and intentional about making improvements, whether they are the result of a network's feedback, a teacher or mentor, or self-assessment. Support learners as they look at feedback; they may need help seeing what is there and responding to the feedback positively and safely (instead of responding defensively, for instance). As the quester works through the actions, explanations, and analyses, some potential answers and actions may begin to illuminate themselves. This is where the learner examines actions' consequences. Potential questions here might include the following.

* What happened?
* How does this impact various factors?
* In what ways does it get me closer to the learning target?
* How do I feel about what happened?
* Does the feedback motivate me, discourage me, pique my curiosity, or intrigue me?

## Begin Again

Once the spiral progresses in a full circle, students are ready to plan and act on the next quest segment. Learners can make one of two moves at this point: (1) develop a new plan or (2) examine the learning target to assess whether it is met or is still germane. Developing a new plan and acting on it includes these potential questions.

* In what ways can this go?

* Whom else might I need to discuss this with?
* What will I do with what I've just learned?
* What is a next step that I am excited about?

The engaging nature of this extended cycle of expertise includes the feeling that one is *so close* to gaining the next level. The learner is always improving and overtly aware of his or her improvement. Everything a quester does is either actively building a new skill, reaping the feel-good benefits of having built up a skill, or facing a new and exciting challenge that clearly requires a new skill or combining already learned skills. In a radio interview with Allison Zmuda (2011), educator Grant Wiggins asserts that if feedback is precise, timely, and nonjudgmental, it is helpful. In the same interview, *Guitar Hero* co-creator Rob Kay says, "Even if the feedback isn't perfect, there is an inherent *stick-to-itiveness*" (Zmuda, 2011). Students see the results of their actions because they see acknowledgment of success and clarity regarding what went wrong, which create an urge to go after it again or take another action. It might materialize as increased experience points, badges, awards, and mastery skill levels, all of which open opportunities in games or visibly improve performance (Alcock, 2014; Sheldon, 2012). *Seeing* progress is important, but so is *feeling* progress.

## Sample Questing Thread

Figure 8.9 shows how the decisions this chapter discussed play out in the disease example questing thread. Again, the document is not completed in its entirety. The form works for elementary, middle, and high school students, though lower grades may require more guidance and, of course, adapting the form to suit students' needs is another option.

We continue to emphasize that these decisions are helpful to guide the work but can also be dynamic and fluid. We continue to consider questions such as, What conversations do we need to have about our plan, or do we need to deviate from our plan? What are we discovering that could impact our deliverables? Have our questions changed? Has our network space changed? and Do we need to try something out in a sandbox zone before our deliverable is finalized?

## Title: We Want to Be as Healthy as Possible as a Community

### Decision Five: Timeline and Action Plan

| Focus: | |
|---|---|
| ✧ Practicing items<br>✧ Assessing networks<br>✧ Identifying and monitoring deliverables' due date | Possible student responses include the following.<br><br>✧ Non-negotiable curriculum items:<br>  ◆ Validating information (two weeks)<br>  ◆ Synthesizing information<br>  ◆ Writing an informational (two weeks)<br><br>✧ Topic items:<br>  ◆ Disease transmission (two weeks)<br>  ◆ Disease prevention (two weeks)<br>  ◆ Connection with community and information sharing (five weeks)<br>  ◆ Modification of information into community QR game (one week)<br>  ◆ Display building (two days over one weekend)<br><br>✧ Question design choices:<br>  ◆ My curriculum essential question is, What is the evidence to support my idea, claim, conclusion, or inference?<br>  ◆ My curriculum driving questions are, To what extent can I currently write an informational about my topic? What would I need to learn to improve my informational? How will I need to modify my informational essay to make it an informational experience for my community?<br>  ◆ My topic essential questions are, How can I better understand how diseases are spread? How can I inspire others to develop and maintain healthy practices that prevent the spread of disease?<br>  ◆ My topic driving question is, To what extent do people have good information about what they need to prevent, minimize exposure to, or treat the disease? How can I help verify and communicate public health messages based on valid scientific information?<br><br>✧ Network design choices:<br>  ◆ I can reach out to the physical and public space to work with the Science Museum of Minnesota about diseases for elementary students and community.<br>  ◆ I can contact the Science Museum of Minnesota by email (travelingexhibits@smm.org) or telephone (651.221.9444). I'll ponder, Can we visit the museum? When could I visit the museum? How much would it cost to take the class to the museum? Can we create one locally? |

Figure 8.9: Considering a timeline and action plan, commitment statements, formative assessment, and feedback for a disease quest.

continued ◆

- I could call the Centers for Disease Control and Prevention at 800.232.4636.
- I could create a QR code informational for the community to learn information about disease spread and preventive measures they can take.
- I can reach out to the museum and offer my feedback and observations of the elementary games.
- I can make a museum with information and tips like the Minnesota one and then put it up here in our community.
- I can solve where we can put the QR codes, how we can let the public know they are there, and whether we should use them over a weekend event or permanently. We'll determine if they should be in the school, park, mall, or town hall and include the name and telephone number of contacts.
✧ Game design choices:
  - I can play the CDC game and document the details about how diseases spread. I can explore the museum game from Michigan and make observations about how it translates the complex information into child-friendly pieces. I can evaluate the accuracy of the museum games using the CDC resources.
  - We can make a game for people to follow locally, like a simulation game with a disease outbreak.
  - I can determine how long it takes to make a QR code and whether it's free to make.

**Timeline and Action Plan**

Twenty-five days (six-week unit)

| Task | Person Responsible | Learning Target | Materials Needed | Time Needed |
|---|---|---|---|---|
| Play CDC games to explore information. | | | | Five days |
| Use museum resources to explore information. | | | | Three days |
| Write on-demand informational on disease spread. | | | | One day |

| Task | Person Responsible | Learning Target | Materials Needed | Time Needed |
|---|---|---|---|---|
| Reach out to community for permission to make informational exhibit or game (school, park, mall, or town hall). | | | | Two hours |
| Check in on contacting process, first essay, amount of information gathered, and validating process. | | | | One day |
| Write feedback to museum based on synthesis. | | | | Two days |
| Get feedback. Check in on quality of feedback letter. | | | | One day |
| Send letter to museum. | | | | One day |
| Send thank-you to CDC for help, if it gave any, after outreach. | | | | Two hours |
| Write second informational on disease using any new information I find. | | | | Two days |
| Check in on final informational, QR code creating, and permission to do exhibit. | | | | One day |
| Design format for final exhibit in space provided and how to make information last for user (QR code, protected paper, and simple signs). | | | | One day |
| Check in for design and format of exhibit and user experience. | | | | One day |
| Modify informational to adapt to the approved design. | | | | One day |
| Set up exhibit. | | | | Two days |
| Survey users for feedback about information and experience. | | | | One day |
| Reflect on feedback. | | | | One day |
| Celebrate! | | | | One day |

continued ◆

| **Decision Six: Commitment Statement** | |
|---|---|
| **Focus:**<br>✧ Commitment language<br>✧ Commitment roles (*I* language and *We* language) | Possible student responses include a signed commitment statement (see Figure 8.2, page 98, and Figure 8.3, page 99). |

| **Decision Seven: Checkpoints** | |
|---|---|
| **Focus:**<br>✧ Purpose<br>✧ Timeline for feedback checkpoints | Possible student responses include the following.<br><br>✧ Reference validity:<br>  ◆ Does the resource include references or links?<br>  ◆ Are there authoritative connections? See the CDC's (n.d.a) *Solve the Outbreak* (http://bit.ly/292UDhu). The CDC is an authoritative source, so I will use that as the most accurate version of the information.<br>✧ People I can reach out to:<br>  ◆ CDC (n.d.b), which provides a list of names and jobs of people willing to be contacts for more information or to share as an affinity space (http://bit.ly/28ZU0mi). I think I can start there to make a connection.<br>  ◆ Science Museum of Minnesota, which has a *Disease Detectives* summary page (www.diseasedetectives.org /about) for more information.<br>✧ Possible assignments we can use to populate content and skills:<br>  ◆ Play the CDC's *Solve the Outbreak* and watch the videos on the *Disease Detectives* exhibit page (www.diseasedetectives.org/videos).<br>  ◆ Compare the videos with the content from the CDC. Ask, "What can we improve for accuracy or clarity?"<br>  ◆ Use this content information to write informational essays about diseases and how to prevent their spread.<br>✧ Checkpoints (six-week quest):<br>  ◆ Check in on contacting process, first essay, amount of information gathered, and validating process (week one).<br>  ◆ Get feedback and check on feedback letter quality (week two).<br>  ◆ Check in on final informational, QR code creating, and permission to do exhibit (week three).<br>  ◆ Consider design elements and check in on logistics for exhibit format (week four).<br>  ◆ Check on design, exhibit format, and user experience (week five).<br>  ◆ Set up exhibit, check in with users for feedback, and reflect on feedback (week six). |

## Decision Eight: Formative Assessment Design

**Focus:**

◇ Targets
◇ Assessment methods for determining feedback
◇ Activities, learning strategies, and checkpoint items

Possible Student Responses:

**Initial Assessment**

| Learning Target | At Standard | Approaching Standard | Notes |
|---|---|---|---|
| I can clearly introduce my topic. | | | |
| I can organize my writing logically. | | | |
| I can select relevant evidence. | | | |
| I can draw conclusions based on the information I find. | | | |
| I can research and examine multiple types of texts to determine what's accurate. | | | |
| I can find and examine sources that identify the spread of the disease and ways to prevent further spread. | | | |
| I can investigate a challenging contemporary global or local issue. | | | |
| I can explore and discover the way that some diseases might be spread. | | | |
| I can seek out misconceptions or fears about how disease spreads and provide accurate information. | | | |

continued ◆

Assessment Reflection:

**Post-Assessment Plan**

| Learning Target | Possible Learning Strategy |
|---|---|
| I can clearly introduce my topic. | |
| I can organize my writing logically. | 1. Use this graphic organizer as a guide to plan for your own essay. <br> 2. Examine this model graphic organizer filled out, and then follow it with your own materials. <br> 3. Work with a friend to read this model essay and deconstruct the logical organization of the model and label each part of the essay. <br> 4. Watch this video on how to organize an essay and then take notes. <br> 5. Create your own learning strategy. |
| I can select relevant evidence. | |
| I can draw conclusions based on the information I find. | |
| I can research and examine multiple types of texts to determine what's accurate. | |
| I can find and examine sources that identify the spread of the disease and ways to prevent further spread. | |
| I can investigate a challenging contemporary global or local issue. | |
| I can explore and discover the way that some diseases might be spread. | |
| I can seek out misconceptions or fears about how disease spreads and provide accurate information. | |

| Decision Nine: Feedback | |
|---|---|
| **Focus:**<br>✧ Feedback timeline<br>✧ Feedback format<br>✧ Feedback audience or source | Possible student responses include the following:<br>✧ Determine if the domain is a mostly trustworthy one, such as .org, .edu, or .gov, or if it is associated with a more questionable domain such as .com, .biz, or .coop. The CDC is .gov, so feel it is a trustworthy one.<br>✧ Create a child-friendly guide to common diseases and their prevention.<br>✧ Get feedback from community using a survey with usefulness and clarity criteria questions.<br>✧ Submit our feedback to museum, and then get feedback from museum after we submit our feedback to them.<br>✧ Synthesize and evaluate disease information.<br>✧ Get information from the CDC on our accuracy (if possible).<br>✧ Participate in peer review with students completing *Disease Detectives* game. (Maybe we can make a chant?)<br>✧ Write informational essay.<br>✧ Get feedback from teacher on informational rubric (three times).<br>✧ Get feedback from friends on informational rubric when they read my essay. |

## Coda

This chapter focused on concrete, familiar instructional aspects (timelines and action plans and checkpoints) and introduced the commitment statement. While these instructional aspects are familiar, the student's role in the development and progress monitoring is a fresh idea. Through scaffolding, teachers invite students to continuously plan, act, evaluate, and reimagine to attack the challenge and master learning targets. This learning partnership empowers students who are navigating sometimes new and potentially difficult terrain to show agency in describing strategies, struggles, and successes.

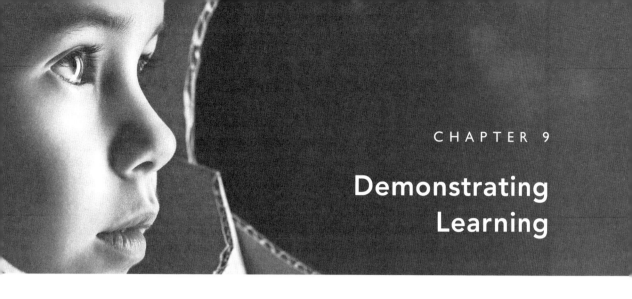

# CHAPTER 9

# Demonstrating Learning

*eliverables*, or products of student learning, are a sort of learning quest souvenir and occur near their culmination. Students develop deliverables to reveal how they frame their ideas, persevere through the process, and master learning targets and curriculum standards. Developing a prototype, organizing and pursuing social reform, or writing a screenplay—all possible deliverables—can take weeks, perhaps months. Working toward these deliverables takes practice. What keeps students going is belief that they can solve an epic problem or challenge if they work hard enough (McGonigal, 2010). Having small skill steps align with clear feedback spirals makes an otherwise overwhelmingly large and complex challenge approachable.

Teachers who guide quests commit to the dual purpose of developing joyful learners and eliciting evidence. This is where Chou's (n.d.) stages of gaming's *endgame* come in. Students reflect on what they experience (most of them with some degree of nostalgia) to help others on the journey or to imagine new adventures. The following sections help teachers guide students while they make deliverable decisions and design endgame experiences. Look back to figure 6.1 (page 68), which centers questing decisions and probing questions around deliverables and closure (or visit **go.SolutionTree.com/instruction** to download the free reproducible "Quest Decisions").

## Deliverable Parameters

In school and work, there is a deadline to meet, a set of expectations by which the teacher or boss evaluates work, and a judgment on the results. The designed deliverable may be an argument the learner writes for a corporation or board of directors, an informational statement for a clinic, a narrative for a game, a whisker plot for some data, or a vocabulary strategies journal. When deciding what deliverable they would like to produce, students get to exhibit immense creativity and initiative. The biggest variable in these evidence types is the person who selects and develops the deliverable and process—the quester. Criteria and unexpected outcomes are both crucial aspects of questing deliverables.

The deliverable should both motivate and measure the learning targets. Before starting students on a quest, decide where you would like to store evidence. Consider digital portfolios or similar tools to help learners organize their evidence. That way, they can reflect on it or use it in the future. You might also store learning evidence and meet checkpoints in Rezzly (http://rezzly.com) or another content-creation platform.

A deliverable must meet three parameters.

1.  It must have established criteria that clarify purpose.
2.  It must take a specific form.
3.  It must have a target audience.

Used in conjunction with checkpoints and the formative assessments chapter 8 (page 97) discussed, figure 9.1 offers reflective prompts for both student and teacher to consider with deliverables.

This figure highlights the student's role as designer and developer. It highlights the student as a person who might consider, "How can I have a role in creating something that matters to me *and* measures non-negotiable criteria?" Teachers entrust students with a seat at the design table to clarify purpose; develop and rework action plans that consider deadlines and access to resources; identify the desired audience and what it expects from them; and provide thoughtful reflection of how the criteria informed the work.

The way you coach during formative assessment—scaffolding appropriately to give students effective practice and paying attention to a specific learning outcome—is not applicable during summative, or deliverable, assessment. Educator and author Grant Wiggins (1998) uses a powerful soccer analogy to describe the difference. In practice, the coach can stop and reteach, provide pointers, engage students in a level of detail, and redo (formative assessment). In the game, the coach is on the sideline, and the students have to deal with the ambiguity or unpredictability of what happens when the situation doesn't go quite according to plan (summative assessment). While the coach can have a few huddles on the sideline to provide advice, students still own the game's outcome.

| Deliverable Components | Student Considerations | Teacher Considerations |
|---|---|---|
| **Purpose:** The desired impact or reason for doing it in the first place | ✧ Why are you doing it?<br>✧ What kind of impact do you want your product or performance to have? | ✧ How can you continue connecting the learning at hand to the bigger goals? |
| **Form:** The physical product or performance based on a genre | ✧ What is the genre, model, or style for your product or performance?<br>✧ How does your product or performance follow the rules of the form?<br>✧ To what extent did you break rules? How might it impact purpose and audience? | ✧ To what extent are students comfortable with the rules of the genre, model, or style?<br>✧ Have you provided enough illustrative examples to result in sharing different approaches with different impacts?<br>✧ How might a checklist's design help guide students' self-direction and conferencing with you? |
| **Audience:** Who is going to view, listen to, play, or experience the form | ✧ Who is going to see it?<br>✧ Is it going to be published or presented to a larger audience?<br>✧ How do you want to engage your audience?<br>✧ What role can your audience have in continuing to make the result better? Do you want to have it play that role? | ✧ What are the requirements for publication (such as a conference, competition, or submission to an outside organization)?<br>✧ How might the checklist design help guide student self-direction and conferencing with you?<br>✧ What are the rules for audience engagement? How can you inform audience members ahead of time to focus their feedback on the learner's goals? |
| **Criteria:** The learning outcomes by which the form and the process are being measured | ✧ How do the key criteria guide your work?<br>✧ Did any unwritten criteria become important to you? | ✧ What does quality look like? How does it directly connect to the learner goals? |

Figure 9.1: Considerations for deliverables.

*Visit go.SolutionTree.com/instruction for a free reproducible version of this figure.*

Note the myriad potential deliverables even in this single example (figure 9.2). This is a new space for teachers to explore as they offer choices to students or co-design with them. Another exciting possibility is that of unexpected outcomes that launch the learning products into unplanned spaces.

| Potential Deliverables | Related Learner Goals: Standards, Contemporary Skills, and Dispositions | Potential Unexpected Outcomes |
|---|---|---|
| Science investigation and conclusion about the given drugs on the market to prevent, cure, or manage a disease | Problem solving | Present to the CDC on research findings. |
| Filmed documentary that humanizes people with the disease and focuses on their daily challenges | Listening with understanding and empathy | Prepare for follow-up if the documentary goes viral, which will prompt additional conversations, methodology defense, the asking and answering of questions, and more; intern at a local walk-in clinic or a nursing home whose patients have the disease the student is studying. |
| Frequently asked questions for a community to calm hysteria and provide information | Practicing expository communication | Adopt FAQ by local city council as part of its emergency preparedness plans. |

Figure 9.2: Deliverable planning.

*Visit **go.SolutionTree.com/instruction** for a free reproducible version of this figure.*

## Student Learning Assessments

Because they are evaluated, deliverables require a scoring tool that aligns with curriculum standards. The tool provides students clarity as they develop their deliverables. You can generate these scoring tools on behalf of or with students. For example, students can write descriptors based on scoring criteria, clarify language so that it makes sense to them, and evaluate sample models to see varying levels of quality.

Identifying key criteria, which the identified goals drive, is crucial. Wiggins and McTighe (2012) offer four key criteria to consider in any task that measure the degree to which students demonstrate conceptual and transferrable knowledge or skill.

1. **Content:** The degree to which the explanation is accurate, clearly explained, complete, expert, and knowledgeable
2. **Process:** The degree to which the work is collaborative, coordinated, efficient, methodical, and precise
3. **Quality:** The degree to which the finished result is creative, organized, polished, effectively designed, and well crafted
4. **Impact:** The degree to which the finished result is entertaining, informative, persuasive, satisfying, and successful

Consider a typical world languages lesson on foods and festivals from regions that speak the target language. That teacher might imagine his or her students creating immersive multimedia experiences for a worldwide audience, perhaps soliciting tourism offices to feature their created content. Figure 9.3 pairs the teacher's quest criteria with American Council on the Teaching of Foreign Languages (ACTFL, n.d.) world-readiness standards. Comparable criteria depend on the topic.

| Identified World-Readiness Standards From ACTFL | Evaluative Quest Criteria |
|---|---|
| **Presentational communication:** Learners present concepts to "inform, explain, persuade, and narrate on a variety of topics using" appropriate media and adapting to various audiences of listeners, readers, or viewers. | ✧ **Content:** Describing, clearly and accurately, for someone who has never been to that restaurant, farm, festival, or market<br>✧ **Process:** Focusing on key details to provide a helpful summary<br>✧ **Quality:** Powerfully using still or moving pictures to feature a given market, restaurant, farm, or festival<br>✧ **Impact:** Understanding how helpful the immersion experience is for tourists |
| **School and global communities:** Learners use the language in the classroom and elsewhere to collaborate within their community and world in general. | ✧ **Content:** Communication with global networks in target language to research as well as offer assistance to a tourism office<br>✧ **Process:** Collaboration with global networks to identify authentic examples<br>✧ **Quality:** Accuracy, clarity, and professionalism in how students communicated with their global network<br>✧ **Impact:** Success of students in offering value to their global network |

*Source for standards: ACTFL, n.d.*

Figure 9.3: Standards and related evaluative criteria.

The essential question—What can we do locally to have an impact globally?—hooked students. This time, the criteria in figure 9.4 connect to school or district learner outcomes and student-friendly learning targets (and also address the possibility of unexpected outcomes). The teacher can draft this figure with students, or students can draft independently with teacher feedback and guidance.

| Quest Connection to School or District Learner Outcomes | Evaluative Criteria Framed as *I Can* Statements |
|---|---|
| **Critical thinking:** Students have to weigh the risks associated with making a financial decision regarding to whom they should loan money. They actively discuss and weigh pros and cons involving cultural values, local traditions, and loan-risk assessment in order to make their ultimate decision. They have to read multiple sources (such as recorded interviews, data tables, infographics, or informational reports) and synthesize the critical information to draw conclusions that impacted the decisions they made. | ✧ **Content:** I can synthesize key information from a variety of sources that may have different points of view. |
| **Global connections:** Students have the opportunity to authentically verify their investigative research while videoconferencing with a teacher (local expert) from the country or countries in which their potential borrowers live. | ✧ **Process:** I can communicate with global partners in a professional manner to discover information. |
| **Collaboration:** Students in each team truly work as one unit. They hold themselves accountable for asking and answering the posed questions pertaining to potential borrowers, especially when studying and analyzing the borrowers' summaries and each investment's potential positive and negative implications. They use web-based tools (like LiveBinders to house curated information and ideas or TodaysMeet to capture online discussions). Students have to come to a team consensus concerning the ultimate borrower they invest in and work collaboratively to generate a meaningful, persuasive piece explaining why the investment for their final candidate is worthwhile. | ✧ **Process:** I can work with my peers to achieve a common goal.<br>✧ **Quality:** I can demonstrate attention to detail in my part of the collaboration.<br>✧ **Impact:** I can listen to my peers, offer ideas, and work to develop a plan that makes me a valued team member. |
| **Communication:** Students write argumentative pieces with a formal claim to describe why they fund a borrower's loan. They can reach consensus concerning the ultimate borrower they invested in and work collaboratively to generate a meaningful, persuasive piece explaining why the investment for their final candidate was worthwhile. | ✧ **Content:** I can develop key claims with supporting evidence that shows the basis of the decision.<br>✧ **Quality:** I can develop a well-crafted argumentative piece, paying attention to organization, grammar, and mechanics. |

| Unexpected outcome: Students decide to extend their giving by creating a schoolwide microloan club. This club creates an initial five-hundred-dollar school portfolio to fund microloans and continues to fund-raise throughout the year to increase the opportunities for global impacts. | ◇ Impact: I can extend my learning outside the classroom when it is meaningful to me. |

Figure 9.4: Learner outcomes and related evaluative criteria.

*Visit **go.SolutionTree.com/instruction** for a free reproducible version of this figure.*

Direct your students to a few websites that you've vetted so, as a class, you can examine illustrative examples of the kinds of deliverables they are considering.

## Reflection

Reflective, mindful sharing about the process focused on celebrating both the wins and the failures along the way is the classic end to the hero's journey. Like Odysseus, students left their comfortable space (receiving and memorizing information) to brave uncharted waters, overcoming predictable and unpredictable challenges. As the learner comes to the end of his or her quest, it helps to reflect on the journey, which does the following.

* It signifies a formal stopping point. Making it to the finish line is an accomplishment itself. Some may need to mourn the end or experience nostalgia for the process.
* It creates a unique moment for reflection on the journey, taking the long view of the dead ends and wrong turns along the way.
* It evaluates the result, including examining how the challenge of the deliverable met the learning goals and unexpected outcomes.
* It celebrates the learning, acknowledging the growth of expert status where appropriate.

In terms of documentation, students may use journals or portfolios to record reflections, feedback, notes, potential shifts in long-term targets, and so on. Within portfolios, students may be saving or sharing resources, conversations on information validity, and feedback from their affinity spaces.

At this point in a quest, learners are burgeoning experts and may celebrate and share their learning—or may be in danger of getting bored with the material. Two things tend to happen simultaneously the moment after the little and big win states are complete: (1) students feel relief that the quest is complete and express readiness for the next unit, and (2) students feel sadness that the commitment to hours of hard work and the network building are ending.

An effective endgame design creates an opportunity for students to continue learning or playing the game long after the class or course moves on to the next unit or the next year. Students can apply the following ideas to reflect on their quests.

* Students generate a blooper reel or present a comedy skit.
* Students write a two-minute drama with characters, build-up, climax, and denouement.
* Students put together a documentary-style presentation.
* Students have a symposium-format discussion comparing quests, identifying similarities, and creating a mural.
* Students construct a guest hall of fame with moments that stand out to them (including scariest, most frustrating, and most joyous moments).

This positive focus will almost certainly send students out into the world ready to learn more.

## Sample Questing Thread

What might a deliverable's plan look like if a student pursuing the disease sample questing thread imagined it to pursue? Elementary, middle, and high school students can brainstorm about deliverable possibilities and potential unexpected outcomes, but lower-level students will require help connecting the related learner goals. Figure 9.2 (page 118) shares a deliverable idea, a connection to related learner goals, and details on how to pursue potential unexpected outcomes.

## Coda

In this chapter, teachers and students decided what those deliverables will look like and what criteria they will follow as part of the endgame phase. Students share their deliverables as teachers conduct a final, summative assessment that measures what matters (curriculum standards, relevant challenges, and increasingly self-directed experiences). Twenty-first century learners face challenges; explore significant topics; discover information outside the traditional methods; learn new skills to solve problems; and create products, demonstrations, and deliverables of value.

With the questing framework, and with the approaches and tools in *The Quest for Learning*, we want to reinvigorate why school matters and how learning can be both strategic and engaging. In short, we hope that what we shared supports improved student learning. It's time to embark. We wish you good fortune on your and your students' future quests.

# Frequently Asked *Quest*ions

Questing is messy learning. To be sure, messy learning is effective. It can be overwhelming to think about open-ended teaching and learning practices that do not have a clearly defined process, but it can also be really exciting—especially for students. True inquiry and high student engagement have long been classroom goals. While many network opportunities and game design elements become intuitive over time, their newness can sometimes be overwhelming. When encountering something new, it is helpful to have readily accessible information. Frequently asked *quest*ions provide quick answers, and that is rare in questing.

## How Can I Help Administrators Understand My Pedagogical Choices?

Instructional decisions require conversation. Communicate with colleagues, with stakeholders (including students), and with administrators—especially at the onset of deciding to engage in a questing instructional framework. Flesh out the online reproducible "Quest Decisions" as much as possible, and take it to curricular or team meetings. (Visit **go.SolutionTree.com/instruction** to download the free reproducible.) Make it clear that educators often build quests on top of existing curricula or unit plans and that these extensions offer authentic opportunities for engaging multiple audiences with divergent tasks and interdependent disciplines. Stress how quests invite high levels of critical thinking, independent and interdependent work, strategic digital media use, and built-in opportunities for connecting globally. Discuss the ethics and safety section in chapter 5 (page 51) to assuage safety concerns.

## How Can I Help My Students Learn to Self-Direct and Fully Participate in the Quest?

An old saying relays two lasting things we can give children: roots and wings (Carter, 1953). Invite them into new models of thinking and learning, and teach them how to deal with the consequences of their choices, how to confidently overcome roadblocks, and how to be strong contributors to help them be good self-directors. Roots modeling should occur often when students are beginning their quest efforts. Teachers gradually release them toward independent behaviors. Wings-enabling coaching and conversation continue throughout, especially if students need reminders about skills, deliverables, and commitments. Becoming comfortable with learner interpretations through student-facing curriculum opportunities is a good first step.

Learning self-direction takes practice. It may take students years to learn to take risks and show courage in their learning. This is acceptable. Greet this delay with support, scaffolding, and models from which students can learn. Think back to the extended cycle of expertise—particularly the part about frustration. We want students to persevere through their quests. To keep them continuously seeking their quest goals, we may need to model what that looks like or reconsider whether a move is a right-sized step.

## How Can I Help Parents See the Benefit of This Type of Instruction?

Again, conversation matters. Because quests are not worksheets and term papers that parents are used to, communication and readiness to address parent trepidation are essential. Let parents know the steps in the process. Share the following with them.

* The list of decisions that students are making (see the reproducible "Quest Decisions" at **go.SolutionTree.com/instruction**)
* The process for developing learning targets and how they might have conversations with their children about meeting those learning targets
* The need to converse with their children about their quests, including how they are progressing, whether they need additional support, and perhaps whether they could offer advice as a mentor or potential affinity space member
* An explanation of affinity spaces and safety
* How they might offer their children feedback about the quest and the steps their children are taking
* Cues to converse with their children about quality so they might habitually ask if their children are doing their best work (and offer support for improving the work when necessary)
* Cues to converse with their children about joy so they might habitually ask about their children's discoveries and explorations and what is exciting them about their learning
* Cues to converse with their children about learning so they can discuss what they are *learning* instead of asking what they are *doing* during the quest.

Offer after-school discussions. Give parents resources for helping their students be effective in their quests. For instance, you can share curated resources online with parents or invite them in as participants or experts in member and mentor spaces. Update them often about progress and areas of improvement. In short, help them help their children in multiple ways, and be mindful of environmental roadblocks like lack of internet access at home and family values and cultures around education in general. Parents might not feel naturally included in school, or might have had a bad school experience themselves. Combat that reticence with invitation, preparation, and celebration. Make sure that parents are part of the win state, whether the wins are small or large.

## How Can I Better Manage My Time When Hosting a Quest?

Quest planning and implementation are shared experiences. Students learn as they help design and engage in their quests. While the prospect of guiding quests may seem overwhelming, answer these two questions when getting started: (1) Where do I begin? and (2) Where do I end? In other words, determine what curriculum or unit plans you will build. Clarify what deliverables or learning you expect.

Consider the usual planning time and set goals within it to lay out organizational decisions. (See chapter 8, page 97, and chapter 9, page 115, for help.) Devote a specific amount of class time to helping students create their timelines, and plan sufficient classroom time for exploration, discovery, feedback, and reflection. Invite parents, co-teachers, media specialists, technology staff, and anybody else willing to lend a hand in your classroom to support students. If quest planning or execution begins taking up more than the affordable time, consider whether all participants are spending their time well and whether students are deeply engaged in the processes. Are students hitting roadblocks or not actively participating? Be ready to offer one-on-one support to move students along or refine a quest. (Use the questions in the reproducible "Quest Decisions" to help you provide support.)

## How Do I Scaffold Quest Elements for Learners With Different Abilities?

Start by acknowledging in class that students learn in different ways. This is one core facet of questing. It helps individualize learning experiences for maximum benefit. When students start creating their plans, the content will likely be easier to interpret than the skills and the deliverable. This is a good opportunity to discuss, perhaps even one-on-one with individual students, multiple levels of skill statements. Refer to student-facing interpretations of teacher-facing skills (see chapter 7, page 89). Students will have their own ideas about how they learn and interact. Be open to their ideas and offer support to keep them on track. Each design choice discussed in this book (inquiry, game, and network) includes multiple levels through which students can move, including different question types, different game types, and different network spaces. You may want to direct students to particular levels to support increasingly sophisticated learning opportunities.

Quests offer students who have giftedness or intrinsic motivation an opportunity for sophistication and enrichment that they may not otherwise encounter. These students may thirst to push beyond the plan's boundaries with sophisticated questions, more intricate network interactions, and fully realized games. Give them the latitude to go as far as they can go.

## How Do I Support Student Choices That Differ From My Own Design Opinions?

Much of the questing experience is about exploring, discovering, and problem solving. Comfortable options handed to the quester don't honor deep student learning. Negotiate but try not to limit students' thinking. If your student's choices are incongruent with yours, pursue critical thinking with a one-on-one conversation. Ask the student to provide a rationale for the choice and for each participant to provide a persuasion attempt. Verbally, together, think through curriculum choices based on the options.

## What Might My School Consider About Its Current Network Spaces?

Physical spaces impact learning's form and design (Jacobs & Alcock, 2017). Does the school have space that allows students to construct models or forms? Is there space to safely and efficiently allow different instructional models to occur simultaneously? It is possible for questing to occur within the traditional classroom. However, it will look and feel different than a quest occurring in a collection of spaces such as communication labs, garages, and small-group collaboration spaces. Spaces that lend themselves to deeper learning because of flexible furniture or multiple types of internet and network access or freedom to move through different physical spaces in school will likely lead to higher-quality work and demonstration of learning.

That said, you have to use what you've got, even if it's a more traditional classroom space with four walls and rows of desks. Consider allowing students to move the desks around or creating stations around the room that utilize different types of seating and different devices for students to use. Be mindful of accessible spaces during planning and design. In *Curriculum 21*, author and editor Heidi Hayes Jacobs (2010) encourages inviting students to "take an architectural walking tour of the school" (p. 75). You can ask them for ideas about how to use existing spaces. This leads to discussion about plus spaces as well. They are critical to opening a quest's range, scope, and connections. Consider additional questions like, Does the school have the bandwidth, devices, and policies in place to support virtual work by learners? What will the school need in terms of physical hardware, software programs, space, and devices? What will it need in terms of policies, procedures, and protocols?

# Quest Decisions

Questing is an instructional framework that offers great flexibility for teachers and students. Despite that open-endedness, quests come with parameters. These probing questions (figure B.1) are for teachers to use with their students while they plan and guide their learning journeys.

| Decision One: Topic or Challenge Criteria | |
|---|---|
| **Focus** | **Probing Questions to Ask Students** |
| ✧ Problem, purpose, challenge, or meaningful idea<br>✧ Non-negotiable learning targets<br>✧ Possible goals and topics of interest | ✧ Why does this matter?<br>✧ How does this relate to daily life for me or people in this place?<br>✧ Which ideas make the most sense and why?<br>✧ Which problems feel familiar? Why?<br>✧ How does this connect to current events?<br>✧ What other problems fit this style or example?<br>✧ What is something you really want to learn more about right now?<br>✧ What would you like to be able to do six weeks from now that you cannot do today?<br>✧ What story do you most often hear yourself telling? What topics do you like talking about?<br>✧ What do you imagine your impact will be years from now?<br>✧ What would you try now if you knew you could not fail?<br>✧ Is there anything else like this?<br>✧ What does this mean to you?<br>✧ How can you solve this problem so it never comes back?<br>✧ Have you thought about the impact you will have by taking on this challenge?<br>✧ How will you transform your life with this new knowledge?<br>✧ What would this mean to you?<br>✧ Which options interest you? |

Figure B.1: Quest decisions.

continued ◆

| | ✧ What is possible? |
| | ✧ What is the dream? |
| | ✧ What is exciting about this to you? |
| | ✧ What other feelings do you have about it? |
| | ✧ What other thoughts do you have about it? |
| | ✧ What is the opportunity here? |
| | ✧ What is the challenge? |
| | ✧ In the bigger picture, how important is this? |

<table>
<tr><td colspan="2" align="center">Decision Two: Question Design</td></tr>
<tr><td>Focus</td><td>Probing Questions to Ask With Students</td></tr>
<tr>
<td>✧ Essential question<br>✧ Driving questions</td>
<td>
✧ What issues or problems do you see here?<br>
✧ Would you elaborate on the purpose of this?<br>
✧ How long have you been thinking about this?<br>
✧ How can you find out?<br>
✧ What will really make the biggest difference here?<br>
✧ Which of your core values does this question express?<br>
✧ Are you approaching this from your head or from your heart?<br>
✧ What do you mean?<br>
✧ What does it feel like?<br>
✧ What is the part that is not yet clear?<br>
✧ What do you want to ask?<br>
✧ What do you want to learn?<br>
✧ Can you tell me more about that?<br>
✧ What other ideas do you have about it?<br>
✧ What other questions do you have about it?<br>
✧ What is here that you want to explore?<br>
✧ What part of the situation have you not yet explored?<br>
✧ What other angles can you think of?<br>
✧ What is just one more possibility?<br>
✧ What are your other options?
</td>
</tr>
<tr><td colspan="2" align="center">Decision Three: Game Design</td></tr>
<tr><td>Focus</td><td>Probing Questions to Ask With Students</td></tr>
<tr>
<td>✧ Play or design<br>✧ Game type<br>✧ Existing games<br>✧ Affinity spaces</td>
<td>
✧ What is your approach to developing the idea?<br>
✧ Tell me what possibilities for action you see, regardless of whether they are realistic.<br>
✧ What possibilities have you seen used?<br>
✧ Which options do you like the most?<br>
✧ How many possibilities can you think of and why?<br>
✧ What options do you choose?<br>
✧ What experience are you looking to create?<br>
✧ How can you enjoy the process of solving this problem?<br>
✧ What story do you want to tell?<br>
✧ How would your ideal self create a solution?<br>
✧ Is this something that you could learn by playing an existing game, or is this something that works better with you as a game designer?
</td>
</tr>
</table>

| | ✧ Would you want to play that game? |
| | ✧ What is your favorite part of this process? |
| | ✧ How would you teach this part? |
| | ✧ Have you ever experienced something like this before? |
| | ✧ How can you improve this idea? |
| | ✧ How can you make this more fun? |
| | ✧ How do you want it to be? |
| | ✧ If you were teaching people how to have fun, what would you say? |

### Decision Four: Network Design

| Focus | Probing Questions to Ask With Students |
|---|---|
| ✧ Physical spaces<br>✧ Plus spaces<br>✧ Public spaces<br>✧ Member spaces<br>✧ Mentor spaces | ✧ Who can help you with this?<br>✧ Whom do you already know in this field?<br>✧ Who needs to know what your plans are?<br>✧ Whom did you help?<br>✧ Who is able to help you?<br>✧ Who else will benefit?<br>✧ Who else would care about this?<br>✧ What is the effect on others?<br>✧ What will you do to get the support you need, and when will you get it?<br>✧ How many possibilities can you think of and why?<br>✧ What do you think about what was said?<br>✧ How would you agree or disagree with this?<br>✧ Are there any similar answers you can think of with alternative routes?<br>✧ How might you convince us that your way is the best way?<br>✧ What resources do you need to help you decide?<br>✧ What do you know about it now?<br>✧ How do you suppose you can find out more about it?<br>✧ What kind of picture do you have right now?<br>✧ What resources are available to you?<br>✧ How do you suppose it will work out?<br>✧ What will that get you?<br>✧ Where will this lead?<br>✧ What are the chances of success?<br>✧ What rules do you need for this?<br>✧ What is the worst thing that can happen? Can you handle that? How would you handle that?<br>✧ How could you have this conversation so it works for everyone?<br>✧ What are they trying to say to you?<br>✧ What are you trying to explain to them?<br>✧ How can you get your needs fully met?<br>✧ Who can answer your question?<br>✧ How can you use this to make it a benefit? |

continued ➧

| | ❖ Are you angry or are you hurt (in response to unfiltered negative feedback)?<br>❖ What are the possibilities?<br>❖ If you had your choice, what would you do?<br>❖ What options can you create? |
|---|---|
| **Decision Five: Timeline and Action Plan** | |
| **Focus** | **Probing Questions to Ask With Students** |
| ❖ Practicing items<br>❖ Assessing networks<br>❖ Identifying and monitoring deliverable's due date | ❖ How much time do you need to do this?<br>❖ How can you learn what you need to know about this?<br>❖ How does this fit with your plans?<br>❖ What do you need to succeed here?<br>❖ Do you have a detailed strategy to get there?<br>❖ What plan do you need in order to achieve your new goals?<br>❖ What details can you add to make this information feel more complete?<br>❖ What is the game plan?<br>❖ What will you have to do to get the job done?<br>❖ What support do you need to accomplish it?<br>❖ What will you do?<br>❖ When will you do it?<br>❖ What do you plan to do about it?<br>❖ What kind of plan do you need to create?<br>❖ How do you suppose you can improve the situation?<br>❖ Now what do you do after it improves?<br>❖ Is this too much?<br>❖ Is there more you can do?<br>❖ What is the first step you can take?<br>❖ When precisely are you going to start and finish each action step?<br>❖ What can arise to make this difficult for you?<br>❖ Is there any part of this you personally don't want to do?<br>❖ How will you work past the external and internal things in your way?<br>❖ Do you need help?<br>❖ What could I do to support you?<br>❖ What is the easiest step you could take?<br>❖ What is the most exciting or interesting step you will take?<br>❖ What are you really looking forward to doing?<br>❖ How much time will this take?<br>❖ What will we do if certain parts do not happen?<br>❖ When will you start?<br>❖ What is holding you back?<br>❖ If I give you an extra hour a day, what will you do with it?<br>❖ Where can we get the time we need to do what we are describing here?<br>❖ Do you mind if I ask a few questions?<br>❖ To what extent does this meet all your objectives? |

| | ✧ Do you have a gut feeling about this?<br>✧ Have you solved a problem like this before?<br>✧ Is this a decision or a pipe dream?<br>✧ Is this goal pulling you forward, or are you struggling to reach it?<br>✧ What is the first step you need to take to reach your goal?<br>✧ How would your life be different if you were able to do this right now?<br>✧ What are the benefits and costs of each option? |
|---|---|
| **Decision Six: Commitment Statement** | |
| **Focus** | **Probing Questions to Ask With Students** |
| ✧ Commitment language<br>✧ Commitment roles (*I* language and *We* language) | ✧ Can you commit to this?<br>✧ What are you willing to commit to here? Anything right now?<br>✧ How do you feel about learning this?<br>✧ How does this decision match up with who you know you are?<br>✧ Is what you are doing here helping you follow your joy?<br>✧ How much energy are you willing to put into that?<br>✧ Is anything holding you back?<br>✧ What are you trying to prove to yourself?<br>✧ Is anything in the way of doing this?<br>✧ What will you have to give up to make room for your goals?<br>✧ What are you willing to do to make this happen?<br>✧ What are you willing to stop doing to make this happen?<br>✧ What do you think will be easy for you?<br>✧ What do you think will be challenging for you?<br>✧ Who do you need to become in order to succeed here?<br>✧ What are you responsible for here?<br>✧ On a scale of one to ten, what commitment level do you need to do this work? What prevents this from being at ten? What could you do to make this commitment closer to ten? |
| **Decision Seven: Checkpoints** | |
| **Focus** | **Probing Questions to Ask With Students** |
| ✧ Purpose<br>✧ Timeline for feedback checkpoints | ✧ What has occurred since we last spoke?<br>✧ What would you like to talk about?<br>✧ When do you need this feedback so you can move forward?<br>✧ What is new (the latest, the update)?<br>✧ How was your week?<br>✧ Where are you right now?<br>✧ What seems to be the main obstacle?<br>✧ What is stopping you?<br>✧ What concerns you the most about _____?<br>✧ What do you want?<br>✧ How have you grown this week?<br>✧ What did you accomplish this week?<br>✧ What are your criteria for success? |

continued ➡

| | |
|---|---|
| | ✧ How will you know if you did the best job you could? |
| | ✧ What is working well? |
| | ✧ In what ways are you moving forward? |
| | ✧ What did you accomplish? |
| | ✧ Have you met any of your goals? To what extent are you on track to meet them? |
| | ✧ Which step are you on right now? |
| | ✧ What are you thinking about right now? |
| | ✧ How are you feeling about your work right now? |
| | ✧ What have you done about this so far? |
| | ✧ What is happening now? What (where, when, who, how much, how often) did you see? |
| | ✧ How can you find out? |
| | ✧ Which set of data or information is most relevant or important? |
| | ✧ How can you justify this information? |
| | ✧ What part of what you just said could be an assumption? |
| | ✧ When will you start? |
| | ✧ Is this goal pulling you forward, or are you struggling to reach it? |
| | ✧ If you don't change this, what will it cost you in the end? |
| | ✧ How can you improve this so it adds value to your work forever? |
| | ✧ How can you learn from this problem so that it never happens again? |
| | ✧ Is this an assumption or have you checked to be sure? |
| | ✧ What results did that produce for you? |
| | ✧ What caused it? |
| | ✧ What led up to it? |
| | ✧ What have you tried so far? |
| | ✧ What do you make of it all? |

| Decision Eight: Formative Assessment Design | |
|---|---|
| **Focus** | **Probing Questions to Ask With Students** |
| ✧ Targets<br>✧ Assessment methods for determining feedback<br>✧ Activities, learning strategies, and checkpoint items | ✧ What do you know already? Are you confident you could show that you know this learning target?<br>✧ How did you feel when you saw how much you knew?<br>✧ What do you feel you can do right now—practice or learn something new?<br>✧ How much energy to learn do you have right now?<br>✧ What do you need to practice?<br>✧ What do you still need to learn?<br>✧ What can you do to practice this specific target?<br>✧ What can you do to learn this specific target?<br>✧ Did that learning strategy work for you in the past?<br>✧ How long do you think it will take to learn this target if you are really working at it?<br>✧ How do you feel about it?<br>✧ Whom could you turn to for help learning this target? |

| | ✧ What small steps can you take to get closer to your goal? |
|---|---|
| | ✧ Will this decision move you forward or keep you stuck? |
| | ✧ Which step would make the biggest difference right now? |
| | ✧ Are your personal standards high enough to reach your goals and targets? |
| | ✧ What does it look like to you? |
| | ✧ What is your assessment? |
| | ✧ What will you take away from this? |
| | ✧ How is this working? |
| | ✧ How would you describe this? |
| | ✧ What do you think this amounts to? |
| | ✧ How would you summarize the effort so far? |
| | ✧ What action will you take? |
| | ✧ What will you do? When? |
| | ✧ Is this a time for action? What action? |
| | ✧ Where do you go from here? When will you do that? |
| | ✧ What are your next steps? By what date or time will you complete these steps? |
| | ✧ If you had free choice in the matter, what would you do? |
| | ✧ If you had it to do over again, what would you do? |

| **Decision Nine: Feedback** | |
|---|---|
| **Focus** | **Probing Questions to Ask With Students** |
| ✧ Feedback timeline<br>✧ Feedback format<br>✧ Feedback audience or source | ✧ What do you want? |
| | ✧ What is your desired outcome? |
| | ✧ If you get it, what will you have? |
| | ✧ How will you know you have reached it? |
| | ✧ What will it look like? How did you determine this to be true? |
| | ✧ Why does that answer make sense to you? |
| | ✧ What am I not asking you that you really want me to ask? |
| | ✧ If you could change just one thing right now, what would it be? |
| | ✧ Is this what you want to work on? |
| | ✧ Are you using this to learn or are you beating yourself up? |
| | ✧ How can you turn this around and have better results next time? |
| | ✧ Is this giving you energy, joy, or happiness or taking it away? |
| | ✧ Are you procrastinating, or is there a reason to delay? |
| | ✧ Have you decided to take action, or are you hoping you will? |
| | ✧ What is holding you back? |
| | ✧ What is missing in the situation? |
| | ✧ Did you do the best job you could? |
| | ✧ On a scale of one to ten, how proud of your work are you right now? (One means not proud at all, and ten means very proud.) |
| | ✧ What is really going on? |
| | ✧ How do you explain this to yourself? |
| | ✧ What was the lesson? |

continued ➡

| | ◆ How can you make sure you remember what you have learned?<br>◆ How would you pull all this together?<br>◆ When do I need this feedback to keep going forward? |
|---|---|
| **Decision Ten: Deliverables** | |
| **Focus** | **Probing Questions to Ask With Students** |
| ◆ Deliverable form<br>◆ Deliverable criteria | ◆ Is this the best outcome you can imagine or is there something greater?<br>◆ What did you learn?<br>◆ Why do you think this works? Does it always work? Why?<br>◆ Is there any way to show exactly what you mean by that?<br>◆ How does that show what you really learned?<br>◆ If you knew the answer, what would it be?<br>◆ How would your ideal self show what was learned?<br>◆ What would you do if you had unlimited resources?<br>◆ What would you like to show others?<br>◆ What really stood out to you through this process? Can you share that with others somehow?<br>◆ What does quality look like? |
| **Decision Eleven: Closure** | |
| **Focus** | **Probing Questions to Ask With Students** |
| ◆ Elements for celebration<br>◆ Elements for next steps<br>◆ Expert confirmation | ◆ What was your biggest win of this process?<br>◆ How will you celebrate that?<br>◆ What did you learn in the process?<br>◆ What does this accomplishment mean to you?<br>◆ How will you use this knowledge to transform your life?<br>◆ What are you grateful for?<br>◆ Who is grateful for you?<br>◆ What could you be happy about?<br>◆ Who did you have to become to achieve it?<br>◆ If you could do it over again, what would you do differently?<br>◆ If it had been you, what would you have done?<br>◆ How else could a person handle this?<br>◆ If you could do anything you wanted, what would you do?<br>◆ To what extent have you changed the world?<br>◆ What is next for you? |

*Visit **go.SolutionTree.com/instruction** for a free reproducible version of this figure.*

# References and Resources

Ahern, L. (2016, June 21). *Using Minecraft to teach math literacy.* Accessed at www.itslearning .eu/using-minecraft-to-teach-math-literacy1 on June 2, 2017.

Aizenman, N. (2015, April 9). *An artist's brainstorm: Put photos on those faceless Ebola suits.* Accessed at www.npr.org/sections/goatsandsoda/2015/04/09/397853271/an-artists -brainstorm-put-photos-on-those-faceless-ebola-suits on May 22, 2017.

Alcock, M. (2012, July). Poster presented at the meeting of CMI.

Alcock, M. (2014). Gaming as a literacy: An invitation. In H. H. Jacobs (Ed.), *Mastering digital literacy* (pp. 79–110). Bloomington, IN: Solution Tree Press.

Alcock, M. (2016, January). Poster presented in Los Gatos, CA.

Alcock, M., Fisher, M., & Zmuda, A. (2015, March). *"INGing" the curriculum: How platforms of questioning, networking, and gaming put learning in students' hands.* Poster presented at the annual meeting of the Association for Supervision and Curriculum Development, Houston, TX.

Alcock, M., Fisher, M., & Zmuda, A. (2017, March). Poster presented at the annual meeting of the 21st Century Learning Conference, Hong Kong.

Alcock, M., Johnson, A., & Sullivan, D. (2012). *Mapping to the Core: Integrating the Common Core Standards into your local school curriculum—Planner.* Salt Lake City, UT: School Improvement Network.

American Association of School Librarians. (2007). *Standards for the 21st century learner.* Chicago: Author.

American Council on the Teaching of Foreign Languages. (n.d.). *World-readiness standards for learning languages.* Accessed at www.actfl.org/sites/default/files/publications/standards /World-ReadinessStandardsforLearningLanguages.pdf on March 20, 2017.

Anyon, J. (1979). Ideology and United States history textbooks. *Harvard Educational Review, 49*(3), 361–386. Accessed at http://hepgjournals.org/doi/10.17763/haer.49.3 .v6m47l352g3hp5j6 on July 8, 2017.

Apple, M. W., & Christian-Smith, L. K. (Eds.). (1991). *The politics of the textbook.* New York: Routledge.

Avenues New York. (n.d.). *Mission: A new school of thought.* Accessed at www.avenues.org/en/nyc/mission on May 14, 2016.

BBC Earth Unplugged. (2013, October 15). *Do animals have feelings?—Earth juice (ep. 46)—Earth Unplugged* [Video file]. Accessed at www.youtube.com/watch?v=9UZizRoQPic on May 21, 2017.

Bereiter, C., & Scardamalia, M. (1993). *Surpassing ourselves: An inquiry into the nature and implications of expertise.* Chicago: Open Court.

Berger, W. (2014). *A more beautiful question: The power of inquiry to spark breakthrough ideas.* New York: Bloomsbury.

Bergmann, J., & Sams, A. (2012). *Flip your classroom: Reach every student in every class every day.* Alexandria, VA: Association for Supervision and Curriculum Development.

Bernard, S. (2010, December 1). *Science shows making lessons relevant really matters.* Accessed at www.edutopia.org/neuroscience-brain-based-learning-relevance-improves-engagement on March 15, 2017.

Black, P., & Wiliam, D. (2009). Developing the theory of formative assessment. *Educational Assessment, Evaluation and Accountability, 21*(1), 5–31.

Bloom, B. S. (Ed.). (1956). *Taxonomy of educational objectives: The classification of educational goals, handbook I—Cognitive domain.* New York: David McKay.

BoardGameGeek. (n.d.a). *Board game: Pandemic » Forums » Strategy.* Accessed at https://boardgamegeek.com/forum/4634/pandemic/strategy on July 20, 2017.

BoardGameGeek. (n.d.b). *Board game: Pandemic Legacy: Season 1 » Forums » General.* Accessed at https://boardgamegeek.com/forum/1539835/pandemic-legacy-season-1/general on July 20, 2017.

BoardGameGeek. (n.d.c). *Subject: Statistics from 2000 games of Pandemic.* Accessed at https://boardgamegeek.com/thread/1591774/statistics-2000-games-pandemic on July 20, 2017.

Bransford, J. D., Brown, A. L., & Cocking, R. R. (Eds.). (2000). *How people learn: Brain, mind, experience, and school.* Washington, DC: National Academy Press.

Breene, K. (2016, January 18). *What is the future of work?* Accessed at www.weforum.org/agenda/2016/01/what-is-the-future-of-work on July 11, 2017.

Cambridge University. (n.d.). *Cambridge Infectious Diseases: Interdisciplinary Research Centre.* Accessed at www.infectiousdisease.cam.ac.uk/schoolzone/games on July 20, 2017.

Carter, H. (1953). *Where Main Street meets the river.* New York: Rinehart.

Centers for Disease Control and Prevention. (n.d.a). *Solve the outbreak.* Accessed at www.cdc.gov/mobile/applications/sto/web-app.html on July 20, 2017.

Centers for Disease Control and Prevention. (n.d.b). *Zika response & success stories.* Accessed at www.cdc.gov/about/24-7/cdcresponders-zika/index.html on July 21, 2017.

Centers for Disease Control and Prevention. (2016). *National health education standards.* Accessed at www.cdc.gov/healthyschools/sher/standards/index.htm on May 26, 2017.

Children's Internet Protection Act of 2000, 47 U.S.C. § 254(1)(B) (2000).

Chou, Y. (n.d.). *Gamification design: 4 phases of a player's journey*. Accessed at http://yukaichou .com/gamification-examples/experience-phases-game on December 20, 2016.

Constitutional Rights: Origins and Travels. (n.d.). *Explore rights around the world*. Accessed at http://constitutionalrights.constitutioncenter.org/app/home/world on July 21, 2017.

Costa, A. L., & Kallick, B. (Eds.). (1995). *Assessment in the learning organization: Shifting the paradigm*. Alexandria, VA: Association for Supervision and Curriculum Development.

Costa, A. L., & Kallick, B. (Eds.). (2000). *Discovering and exploring habits of mind*. Alexandria, VA: Association for Supervision and Curriculum Development.

Crockett, L. W., & Churches, A. (2017). *Growing global digital citizens: Better practices that build better learners*. Bloomington, IN: Solution Tree Press.

Davachi, L., Kiefer, T., Rock, D., & Rock, L. (2010). Learning that lasts through AGES. *NeuroLeadership Journal*, *3*, 1–11.

Demolliens, M., Isbaine, F., Takerkart, S., Huguet, P., & Boussaoud, D. (2017). Social and asocial prefrontal cortex neurons: A new look at social facilitation and the social brain. *Social Cognitive and Affective Neuroscience*, 1–8. Accessed at www.ncbi.nlm.nih.gov/ pubmed/28402489 on July 9, 2017.

Depka, E. (2017). *Raising the rigor: Effective questioning strategies and techniques for the classroom*. Bloomington, IN: Solution Tree Press.

Dewey, J. (1916). *Democracy and education: An introduction to the philosophy of education*. New York: Macmillan.

Durst, B. (2015, May 2). Innovative power of asking, "What if? Why not? & So what?". Accessed at https://formofthegood.wordpress.com on September 13, 2017.

Evans, M., & Boucher, A. R. (2015). Optimizing the power of choice: Supporting student autonomy to foster motivation and engagement in learning. *Mind, Brain, and Education*, *9*(2). Accessed at https://eric.ed.gov/?id=EJ1060256 on March 15, 2017.

Fawcett, L. M., & Garton, A. F. (2005). The effect of peer collaboration on children's problem-solving ability. *British Journal of Educational Psychology*, *75*(2), 157–169. Accessed at http://onlinelibrary.wiley.com/doi/10.1348/000709904X23411/full on June 30, 2017.

Ferguson, C. J., Brown, J. M., & Torres, A. V. (2016). *Education or indoctrination? The accuracy of introductory psychology textbooks in covering controversial topics and urban legends about psychology*. Accessed at www.christopherjferguson.com/Education%20or%20 Indoctrination.pdf on July 8, 2017.

Fisher, M. (2013). *Digital learning strategies: How do I assign and assess 21st century work?* Alexandria, VA: Association for Supervision and Curriculum Development.

Fisher, M. (2015). *Ditch the daily lesson plan: How do I plan for meaningful student learning?* Alexandria, VA: Association for Supervision and Curriculum Development.

Fisher, M., & Tolisano, S. R. (2014). Digital masters: Becoming a blogmaster, annotexter, or web curator. In H. H. Jacobs (Ed.), *Mastering digital literacy* (pp. 5–26). Bloomington, IN: Solution Tree Press.

Gallup. (2016, Fall). *Gallup student poll: Engaged today—Ready for tomorrow*. Accessed at www.gallupstudentpoll.com/197492/2016-national-scorecard.aspx on March 15, 2017.

GamesDreams. (n.d.). *Play Pandemic: The Board Game game online—Pandemic: The Board Game.* Accessed at http://gamesdreamsonline.com/showthread.php?234679 -Play-Pandemic-The-Board-Game-Game-Online on July 6, 2017.

Gapminder. (n.d.). *Dollar Street.* Accessed at www.gapminder.org/dollar-street/matrix ?thing=Toys&countries=World&regions=World&zoom=4&row=1&lowIncome =26&highIncome=15000&lang=en on July 11, 2017.

Gee, J. P. (2007). *Good video games and good learning: Collected essays on video games, learning, and literacy.* New York: Peter Lang.

Gee, J. P., & Hayes, E. R. (2011). *Language and learning in the digital age.* New York: Routledge.

Global Digital Citizen Foundation. (n.d.). *Global digital citizen.* Accessed at https:// globaldigitalcitizen.org/21st-century-fluencies/global-digital-citizenship on July 11, 2017.

Godin, S. (2010). *Linchpin: Are you indispensable?* New York: Portfolio.

Hanover Research. (2014, August). *The impact of formative assessment and learning intentions on student achievement.* Accessed at www.hanoverresearch.com/media/The-Impact-of-Formative -Assessment-and-Learning-Intentions-on-Student-Achievement.pdf on May 21, 2017.

Haskell, C. (2012). *Design variables of attraction in quest-based learning* (Unpublished doctoral dissertation). Boise State University, Boise, Idaho. Accessed at http://works.bepress.com /chris_haskell/14 on December 30, 2014.

Hobson, N. M., & Inzlicht, M. (2016). The mere presence of an outgroup member disrupts the brain's feedback-monitoring system. *Social Cognitive and Affective Neuroscience, 11*(11), 1698–1706. Accessed at www.ncbi.nlm.nih.gov/pmc/articles/PMC5091674 on December 4, 2016.

Interactive Educational Systems Design. (2014). *Small-business edition: 2014 national survey on mobile technology for K–12 education.* Accessed at www.stemreports.com/products-page /market-research/business-edition-2013-national-survey-on-mobile-technology-for-k-12 -education-1-20-readers on July 19, 2017.

Jacobs, H. H. (Ed.). (2010). *Curriculum 21: Essential education for a changing world.* Alexandria, VA: Association for Supervision and Curriculum Development.

Jacobs, H. H., & Alcock, M. (2017). *Bold moves for schools: How we create remarkable learning environments.* Alexandria, VA: Association for Supervision and Curriculum Development.

Kallick, B., & Alcock, M. (2013). A virtual continuum for thinking interdependently. In A. L. Costa & P. W. O'Leary (Eds.), *The power of the social brain: Teaching, learning, and interdependent thinking* (pp. 49–60). New York: Teachers College Press.

Kallick, B., & Zmuda, A. (2017a). Orchestrating the move to student-driven learning. *Educational Leadership, 74*(6), 53–57.

Kallick, B., & Zmuda, A. (2017b). *Students at the center: Personalizing learning with habits of mind.* Alexandria, VA: Association for Supervision and Curriculum Development.

Klein, B. (2009, January 31). *Commitment statements.* Accessed at http://collaborationking .com/collaboration-exercises/2009/1/31/commitment-statements.html on July 30, 2016.

Kolb, D. A. (1984). *Experiential learning: experience as the source of learning and development.* Englewood Cliffs, NJ: Prentice Hall.

Kotler, P., & Lee, N. R. (2008). *Social marketing: Influencing behaviors for good* (3rd ed.). Thousand Oaks: SAGE.

Lambert, J., & Ennis, J. (2014). Quest-based learning: A new approach to preservice teacher technology instruction. In M. Searson & M. Ochoa (Eds.), *Proceedings of Society for Information Technology and Teacher Education International Conference 2014* (pp. 2895–2900). Chesapeake, VA: Association for the Advancement of Computing in Education.

Lambert, J., Gong, Y., & Harrison, R. (2016). Autonomous, self-paced quest-based learning: Is it more motivating than traditional course instruction? In G. Chamblee & L. Langub (Eds.), *Proceedings of Society for Information Technology and Teacher Education International Conference 2016.* Chesapeake, VA: Association for the Advancement of Computing in Education.

Marzano, R. J. (2003). *What works in schools: Translating research into action.* Alexandria, VA: Association for Supervision and Curriculum Development.

Marzano, R. J. (Ed.). (2010). *On excellence in teaching.* Bloomington, IN: Solution Tree Press.

Marzano, R. J. (2017). *The new art and science of teaching.* Bloomington, IN: Solution Tree Press.

McCrindle. (2014). *Generation Z: Born 1995–2009.* Accessed at http://mccrindle.com.au/resources/Gen-Z-Claire-Madden_Infographic_McCrindle.pdf on February 1, 2016.

McEvers, K. (2016, November 22). *Stanford study finds most students vulnerable to fake news.* Accessed at www.npr.org/2016/11/22/503052574/stanford-study-finds-most-students-vulnerable-to-fake-news on June 1, 2017.

McGonigal, J. (2010, February). *Jane McGonigal: Gaming can make a better world* [Video file]. Accessed at www.ted.com/talks/jane_mcgonigal_gaming_can_make_a_better_world/transcript
?language=en#t-43278 on February 2, 2017.

McLeod, S. (2016, March 16). *The biggest indictment of our schools is not their failure to raise test scores.* Accessed at http://dangerouslyirrelevant.org/2016/03/the-biggest-indictment-of-our-schools-is-not-their-failure-to-raise-test-scores.html on May 23, 2017.

McTighe, J., & Curtis, G. (2015). *Leading modern learning: A blueprint for vision-driven schools.* Bloomington, IN: Solution Tree Press.

McTighe, J., & Wiggins, G. (2013). *Essential questions: Opening doors to student understanding.* Alexandria, VA: Association for Supervision and Curriculum Development.

Mitra, S. (2010, July). *The child-driven education* [Video file]. Accessed at www.ted.com/talks/sugata_mitra_the_child_driven_education on May 26, 2017.

National Coalition for Core Arts Standards. (2012). *National Core Arts standards: A conceptual framework for arts learning.* Accessed at www.nationalartsstandards.org/content/conceptual-framework on June 22, 2017.

National Council for the Social Studies. (2013). *College, career and civic life (C3) framework for social studies state standards: Guidance for enhancing the rigor of K–12 civics, economics, geography, and history.* Silver Spring, MD: Author.

National Governors Association Center for Best Practices & Council of Chief State School Officers. (2010a). *College and career readiness anchor standards for speaking and listening.* Accessed at www.corestandards.org/ELA-Literacy/CCRA/SL on July 6, 2017.

National Governors Association Center for Best Practices & Council of Chief State School Officers. (2010b). *Common Core State Standards for English language arts and literacy in history/social studies, science, and technical subjects.* Washington, DC: Authors. Accessed at www.corestandards.org/assets/CCSSI_ELA%20Standards.pdf on July 11, 2017.

National Governors Association Center for Best Practices & Council of Chief State School Officers. (2010c). *Common Core State Standards for mathematics.* Washington, DC: Authors. Accessed at www.corestandards.org/wp-content/uploads/Math_Standards1.pdf on July 11, 2017.

National Institute of Diabetes and Digestive and Kidney Diseases. (2013, September). *Pancreatic islet transplantation.* Accessed at www.niddk.nih.gov/health-information/diabetes/overview/insulin-medicines-treatments/pancreatic-islet-transplantation on May 23, 2017.

National Research Council. (1990). *Reshaping school mathematics: A philosophy and framework for curriculum.* Washington, DC: National Academy Press.

National Research Council. (2012). *A framework for K–12 science education: Practices, crosscutting concepts, and core ideas.* Washington, DC: National Academies Press.

Nebel, S., Schneider, S., & Rey, G. D. (2016). From duels to classroom competition: Social competition and learning in educational videogames within different group sizes. *Computers in Human Behavior, 55,* 384–398.

Next Generation Science Standards Lead States. (2013). *Next Generation Science Standards: For states, by states.* Washington, DC: National Academies Press.

Nilson, L. B. (2013). *Creating self-regulated learners: Strategies to strengthen students' self-awareness and learning skills.* Sterling, VA: Stylus.

Orf, D. (2013, August 12). *8 superpowers brought to you by technology.* Accessed at www.popular mechanics.com/technology/g1258/8-superpowers-brought-to-you-by-technology on July 11, 2017.

Organisation for Economic Co-operation and Development. (2012). *Compare your country: PISA digital skills.* Accessed at www.oecd.org/education/students-computers-and-learning -9789264239555-en.htm on March 15, 2017.

Packard, E. (n.d.). *A brief history of Choose Your Own Adventure.* Accessed at www.edwardpackard .com/cyoa.php on March 9, 2017.

Partnership for 21st Century Learning. (n.d.). *Framework for 21st century learning.* Accessed at www.p21.org/about-us/p21-framework on March 15, 2017.

Partnership for 21st Century Learning. (2016). *What we know about collaboration: Part of the 4Cs Research Series.* Accessed at www.p21.org/storage/documents/docs/Research/P21_4Cs _Research_Brief_Series_-_Collaboration.pdf on July 9, 2017.

Posselt, J. R., & Lipson, S. K. (2016). Competition, anxiety, and depression in the college classroom: Variations by student identity and field of study. *Journal of College Student Development, 57*(8), 973–989.

Project Tomorrow. (2013). *The new digital learning playbook: Mobile learning*. Accessed at www.tomorrow.org/speakup/pdfs/SU2013_MobileLearning.pdf on March 15, 2017.

Rosling, H. (2006, February). *Hans Rosling: The best stats you've ever seen* [Video file]. Accessed at www.ted.com/talks/hans_rosling_shows_the_best_stats_you_ve_ever_seen on May 21, 2017.

Rowe, P. G. (1987). *Design thinking*. Cambridge: Massachusetts Institute of Technology Press.

Safina, C. (2015, October). *Carl Safina: What are animals thinking and feeling?* [Video file]. Accessed at www.ted.com/talks/carl_safina_what_are_animals_thinking_and_feeling on May 21, 2017.

Schell, J. (2015). *The art of game design: A book of lenses* (2nd ed.). Boca Raton, FL: CRC Press.

ScienceGameCenter. (n.d.). *Games: All games—Dealing with disease*. Accessed at www.sciencegamecenter.org/games?subject=disease on July 20, 2017.

Scott, D., & Marzano, R. J. (2014). *Awaken the learner: Finding the source of effective education*. Bloomington, IN: Marzano Research.

Sheldon, L. (2012). *The multiplayer classroom: Designing coursework as a game*. Boston: Course Technology.

Squire, K. (2011). *Video games and learning: Teaching and participatory culture in the digital age*. New York: Teachers College Press.

STEMReports. (2014, June 22). *Promising practices for student learning*. Accessed at www.stemreports.com/promising-practices-for-student-learning on April 14, 2017.

Stevens, A. P. (2014, September 2). Learning rewires the brain. *Science News for Students*. Accessed at www.sciencenewsforstudents.org/article/learning-rewires-brain on March 17, 2017.

Stiggins, R. (2017). *The perfect assessment system*. Alexandria, VA: Association for Supervision and Curriculum Development.

Stiggins, R., Arter, J., Chappuis, J., & Chappuis, S. (2007). *Classroom assessment for student learning: Doing it right—Using it well*. Upper Saddle River, NJ: Pearson.

Swift, J. N., & Gooding, C. T. (1983). Interaction of wait time feedback and questioning instruction on middle school science teaching. *Journal of Research in Science Teaching, 20*(8), 721–730.

Talbot, M. (2015, January 9). A quest for a different learning model: Playing games in school. *The Hechinger Report*. Accessed at http://hechingerreport.org/content/quest-different-learning-model-playing-games-school_18465 on March 8, 2016.

The United States Conference of Catholic Bishops. (n.d.). *The stack of the deck: An illustration of the root causes of poverty*. Accessed at www.usccb.org/about/justice-peace-and-human-development/stack-of-the-deck.cfm on May 21, 2017.

Vista Innovation and Design Academy. (n.d.). *Our values (GILLS)*. Accessed at http://vida.vistausd.org/gills on February 2, 2017.

Wagner, T. (2008). Rigor redefined. *Educational Leadership, 66*(2), 20–25.

Wagner, T. (2010). *The global achievement gap: Why even our best schools don't teach the new survival skills our children need—And what we can do about it*. New York: Basic Books.

Wiggins, G. (1998). *Educative assessment: Designing assessments to inform and improve student performance.* San Francisco: Jossey-Bass.

Wiggins, G. (2013, May 1). *The Common Core Standards: A defense* [Blog post]. Accessed at https://grantwiggins.wordpress.com/2013/05/01/the-common-core-standards-a-defense on July 22, 2016.

Wiggins, G., & McTighe, J. (1998). *Understanding by design.* Alexandria, VA: Association for Supervision and Curriculum Development.

Wiggins, G., & McTighe, J. (2005). *Understanding by design* (Expanded 2nd ed.). Alexandria, VA: Association for Supervision and Curriculum Development.

Wiggins, G., & McTighe, J. (2012). *The understanding by design guide to advanced concepts in creating and reviewing units.* Alexandria, VA: Association for Supervision and Curriculum Development.

Willis, J. (2011, October 5). *Three brain-based teaching strategies to build executive function in students* [Blog post]. Accessed at www.edutopia.org/blog/brain-based-teaching-strategies-judy-willis on December 8, 2016.

Willis, J. (2016, May 3). *Judgment: Navigating choices and decisions* [Blog post]. Accessed at www.edutopia.org/blog /judgment-navigating-choices-and-decisions-judy-willis on November 6, 2016.

Winter, J. M. (2015). *How hope and motivation lead to self-regulation in middle school students* (Master's capstone paper). St. Paul, MN: Hamline University. Accessed at http:// digitalcommons.hamline.edu/cgi/viewcontent.cgi?article=1276&context=hse_all on February 2, 2017.

Wright, W. (2007, March). *Will Wright: Spore, birth of a game* [Video file]. Accessed at www.ted .com/talks/will_wright_makes_toys_that_make_worlds on April 19, 2017.

Zimmerman, E. (2011). *Gaming literacy: Game design as a model for literacy in the twenty-first century.* Accessed at http://ericzimmerman.com/files/texts/Chap_1_Zimmerman.pdf on December 8, 2016.

Z-Man Games [ZManGamesOfficial]. (n.d.). Pandemic [YouTube channel]. Accessed at www.youtube.com/user/ZManGamesOfficial/videos on July 20, 2017.

Zmuda, A. (Host). (2011). *Masterful feedback drives vigorous learning* [Audio file]. Accessed at www.jackstreet.com/jackstreet/hWSAC.KayWiggins.cfm on June 16, 2016.

Zmuda, A., Curtis, G., & Ullman, D. (2015). *Learning personalized: The evolution of the contemporary classroom.* San Francisco: Jossey-Bass.

Zull, J. E. (2002). *The art of changing the brain: Enriching the practice of teaching by exploring the biology of learning.* Sterling, VA: Stylus.

# Index

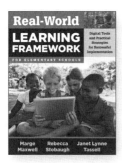

### Real-World Learning Framework for Elementary Schools
**_Marge Maxwell, Rebecca Stobaugh, and_**
**_Janet Lynne Tassell_**
Bring about deeper, self-directed learning in elementary school students through real-world project-based instruction to help students partner in their own learning.
**BKF753**

### Real-World Learning Framework for Secondary Schools
**_Marge Maxwell, Rebecca Stobaugh, and_**
**_Janet Lynne Tassell_**
Discover how to use the Create Excellence Framework to help students find greater fulfillment in learning, while also meeting the guidelines of curriculum standards.
**BKF656**

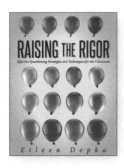

### Raising the Rigor
**_Eileen Depka_**
This user-friendly resource shares questioning strategies and techniques proven to enhance students' critical-thinking skills, deepen their engagement, and better prepare them for college and careers. The author also provides a range of templates, surveys, and checklists for planning instruction, deconstructing academic standards, and increasing classroom rigor.
**BKF722**

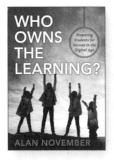

### Who Owns the Learning?
**_Alan November_**
Learn how to harness students' natural curiosity to help them develop into self-directed learners. Discover how technology allows students to take ownership of their learning, create and share learning tools, and participate in work that is meaningful to them and others.
**BKF437**

## Solution Tree | Press
a division of
Solution Tree

Visit SolutionTree.com or call 800.733.6786 to order.

# GL⬤BAL **PD**

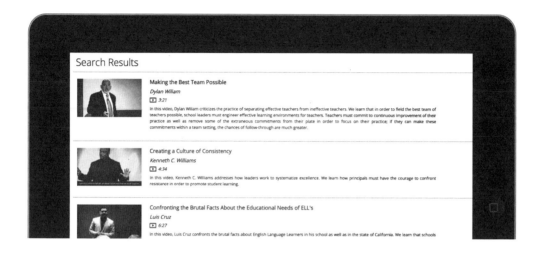

# Access **Hundreds of Videos & Books** from Top Experts

**Global PD** gives educators focused and goals-oriented training from top experts. You can rely on this innovative online tool to improve instruction in every classroom.

- Gain job-embedded PD from the largest library of PLC videos and books in the world.

- Customize learning based on skill level and time commitments; videos are less than 20 minutes, and books can be browsed by chapter to accommodate busy schedules.

- Get unlimited, on-demand access—24 hours a day.

▶ **LEARN MORE**

SolutionTree.com/GlobalPDLibrary

Solution Tree